CHOOSE HARD LIVE EASY

The Commander's Official Companion Workbook

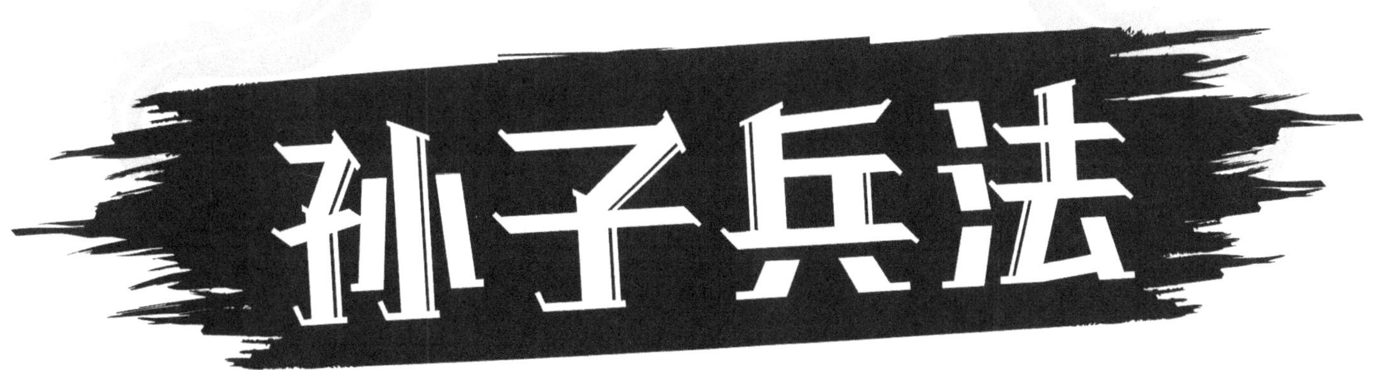

Master the Art of War for Decision-Making with 50+ Live Combat Exercises

MJ DeMARCO

INTERNATIONAL BEST-SELLING AUTHOR OF THE MILLIONAIRE FASTLANE

Workbook ISBN: 979-8-9942338-0-1
Paperback ISBN: 978-1-7367924-6-9
Kindle ISBN: 978-1-7367924-7-6
Audiobook ISBN: 978-1-7367924-8-3
Hardback ISBN: 978-1-7367924-5-2

The information presented herein represents the view of the author as of the date of publication. This book is presented for informational purposes only. Under no circumstances should any idea, strategy, or concept in this book be construed as financial or health advice. Due to the rate at which conditions change, the author reserves the right to alter and update his opinions based on new conditions. While every attempt has been made to verify information in the book, neither the author or his affiliates, partners, or licensees assume any responsbility for errors, inaccuraacies, or omissions.

Published by Viperion Publishing Corporation
5513 W 11000 N #161
Highland UT, 84003

For license inquiries or bulk buying options, please contact the publisher at https://www.viperionpublishing.com or support@viperionpublishing.com

Table of Contents

Introduction 4

Chapter 1: The Combat Battlefield.. 7

Chapter 2: The Armory of Decision Weapons... 8

Chapter 3: The Decision Gauntlet.. 13

Chapter 4: The Invisible Witness... 19

Chapter 5: Your Decisional Fallout Condition (DEFCON) and Your Likely Future..... 25

Chapter 6: Your Decisional Situation Report (Are You Winning or Losing?)................ 28

Chapter 7: The Pastor in the Parking Lot... 32

Chapter 8: The Benevolent Burglars.. 35

Chapter 9: The Unwritten Future... 44

Chapter 10: Hack the Kitchen... 54

Chapter 11: A Backcasted Best Life... 56

Chapter 12: XMAS at the Coffee Shop... 60

Chapter 13: The Uncomfortable Comfort Zone... 65

Chapter 14: Time Share Vacation Bliss.. 72

Chapter 15: The Myth of the Natural... 74

Chapter 16: The High School Reunion.. 79

Chapter 17: The "FOMO" Counterfeit Hard.. 83

Chapter 18: The Curse of Expectosis... 88

Chapter 19: Strategic Gratitude.. 91

Chapter 20: The Prisoner's Dilemma (Job or Financial?)............................ 93

Chapter 21: The Prison Walls That Jail Us.. 102

Chapter 22: The Vampire Retainer... 108

Chapter 23: The Digital Heist.. 112

Chapter 24: The Family First Guilt Trip.. 112

Chapter 25: The "Sucks" Subscription You Didn't Want............................ 116

Chapter 26: The "I Deserve It" Trap... 117

Chapter 27: Juggling Zeroes and Lit Dynamite... 119

Chapter 28: The Walking Dead: Origin Story.. 123

Chapter 29: Operation Red Pill... 126

Appendix A: Your Decision Armory.. 130

Appendix B: Behavioral Index of Decision Weapons.................................. 131

Appendix C: Choose Hard, Live Easy Visual Cheatsheets........................... 136

Appendix D: WADM Worksheets.. 139

Appendix E: Kaizen Scorecards... 142

Appendix F: Willpower Bootcamp Checklists.. 146

Appendix G: Backcasting "To Do" Lists.. 150

Appendix H: Dice Appendix - Chaos Outcomes... 154

Introduction
Welcome to the Art of War for Decision-Making.

The war for your best or worst life.

If you're armed with this workbook, it means you are done with theory and ready for execution. This companion workbook integrates concepts *Choose Hard, Live Easy: The Art of War for Decision-Making* by MJ DeMarco, and fuses them into your daily operating system.

My objective is to normalize strategic decision-making, beyond mere thoughts or reflections, but install routine paradigms for living that become as automatic as sleeping.

"Worst You" is killed off; "Best You" thrives. Success and happiness are the spoils. Here's how to begin...

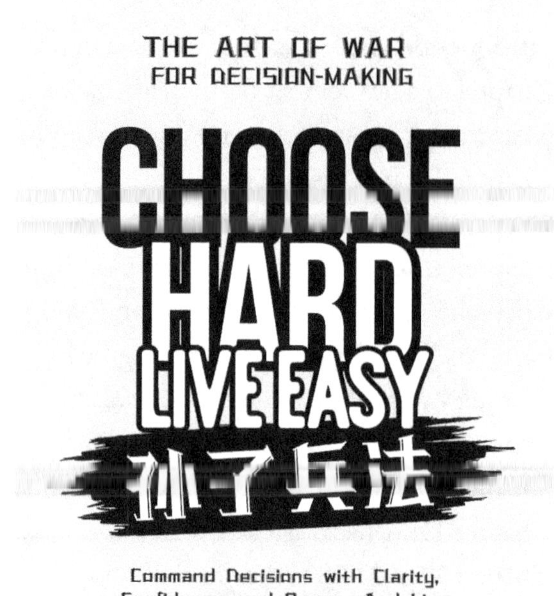

1) SURVIVE DECISION COMBAT TRAINING
This workbook is the official companion to the main feature-length book, *Choose Hard, Live Easy— The Art of War for Decision-Making: Command Decisions with Clarity, Confidence, and Live Like a King Who Conquered.*

It is highly recommended you read the main book as it gives you expertise to master decision combat. It is the "Why" and the "How," providing the philosophical and mental armor you need to survive the battle. While you can apply the tools and tactics in this book without the preface of the main book, it will put you at a disadvantage... like entering a sword duel while never swinging a sword.

2) REQUIRED HARDWARE: A PAIR OF SIX-SIDED DICE
Life (and decision-making) is a mix of strategy and probability. You can make the perfect choice and still get hit by a bus. To simulate life's chaos and unpredictability of real-world decision-making, get yourself a pair of standard six-sided dice. Throughout this manual, you will face scenarios where a roll of the dice will give you the outcome. Some great decisions might yield poor outcomes, and vice versa. As you will learn, strategic decision making is judged by the process through which they are made— not the outcomes. We choose, roll the dice, and face the consequences—just like in the real world.

3) THE COMBAT MODULES

This workbook is organized into different modules, each representing a different form of combat training. Each type of module is prefixed with an icon to prepare you into the drill.

This symbol gives you the background intelligence about the decision concept that follows.

This symbol indicates a hypothetical story with a pending decision. Read carefully. Decide carefully.

This represents a training exercise that you will need to execute in the real world with real world implications.

This symbol indicates a critical piece of decision intelligence that you should carry with you for a lifetime.

This represents a mental exercise that you requires honest reflection... on your past, or your future.

This symbol indicates deliberate strategy, planning, and thought exercises. Embrace the process.

This means it is time to roll your dice and get a random outcome for your decision. Chaos, unleashed. Results variable.

4) CONCEPT REFRESHER

The following terms are used throughout this workbook. Below is a short refresher.

- The Shadow War: The war between Hard and Easy, "Best You" versus "Worst You" governed by the Easy/Hard paradox.
- Campaign Decisions: Long-term committed decisions requiring discipline & flow (habits).
- Frontier Decisions: Sudden life pivots (Job/career changes, moving, marriage/divorce)
- Combat Decisions: Daily decisions that seem inconsequential (eating, driving, free time)
- Treason Decisions: Easy/poor decisions that ripple through time, immediately or compounded.
- Power Decisions: Hard/good decisions that ripple through time, immediately or compounded.
- Flow Decisions: Hard/Easy decisions that compound into habits.
- The Royal Guard of Happiness: Health, Freedom, Relationships, Spirituality, Meaning/Purpose.
- Asymmetry: The idea of lopsided gambles; for example, gambling one dollar to win one penny (downside).
- The Hard Choice Flywheel: The process of Choosing Hard; absolute responsibility, episodic courage, routine discipline, momentary discomfort.

5) DO THE WORK– LIVE THE SPOILS

Let's get one thing straight before you turn the page: This workbook is inanimate. It has no heartbeat, no discipline, and no willpower. It cannot drag you out of bed, it cannot make you fire a toxic client, and it sure as hell cannot force you to Choose Hard.

Right now, this is just a stack of paper and ink. You are the engine.

The brutal honesty you pour into these margins is what transforms a worthless pile of pulp into a lethal arsenal for living. This manual is only as effective as the hands that hold it. My objective isn't to give you a place to doodle. It's to permanently rewire your cognitive hard drive. I want these frameworks—more than 50 of them—seared into your psyche so deeply that calculating your next move becomes as automatic as breathing, blinking, or bathing.

I won't insult your intelligence with guru guarantees. I can't promise that filling out these boxes will magically teleport you to your dream life. **But I can guarantee the math**. If you do the reps, you radically manipulate the probabilities in your favor—nuking the odds of a life you hate, and realistically engineering the life you want. Everything you want from life is always a few Hard choices away.

Let the games begin. The simulation is live. Your choices are the joystick.

The Cartel is waiting to enslave you. Choosing Hard is hoping to free you.

As with everything in the Shadow War, the next play belongs to you.

Your choice.
Your move.
Your life.

MJ DeMarco, Author,
Choose Hard, Live Easy: The Art of War for Decision-Making

Chapter 1
The Combat Battlefield

THE 4 RULES OF DECISION ENGAGEMENT

The Easy/Hard Paradox and decision combat is governed by 4 Rules of Engagement and 5 Laws of Decision Power. Your life's enduring reality is a result of these paradigms. Those who recognize how decisions flow into their frameworks will win life.

- **Polarity**: Whatever you choose—Easy or Hard—you eventually get its opposite in return.
- **Transcience**: Whatever you choose, its joy (Easy) or its (Pain) will be temporary and fleeting.
- **Persistence**: Whatever you choose, it's opposite from polarity will persist as a state of existence.
- **Imminence**: Hard is inevitable & cannot be avoided. Choose Hard *now*, or have Hard choose you *later*.

THE 5 LAWS OF DECISION POWER
Decision Power flows through the Hourglass of Lifespan.

- **The Law of Momentality—The Axis of Power:** The epicenter of all decisions. Your entire life can be summarized in one moment, the present, and that it is the singularity where all your decisions are made or not made. Life is lived here.
- **The Law of Pastuality—The Mod of Power:** Our memories and experiences can either serve or sabotage Momentality. This is also a decision.
- **The Law of Eventuality—The Aftermath of Power:** The powerful aftermath of our decisions where the consequences are either suffered, or enjoyed.
- **The Law of Inevitability—The End of Power:** Death is only one moment, and it is our last moment, the final end of Power.
- **The Law of Asymmetry—The Magnitude of Power:** The explosive impact of our decisions that can reverberate through the months, years, and decades. Asymmetry is life's defining (or wrecking) force.

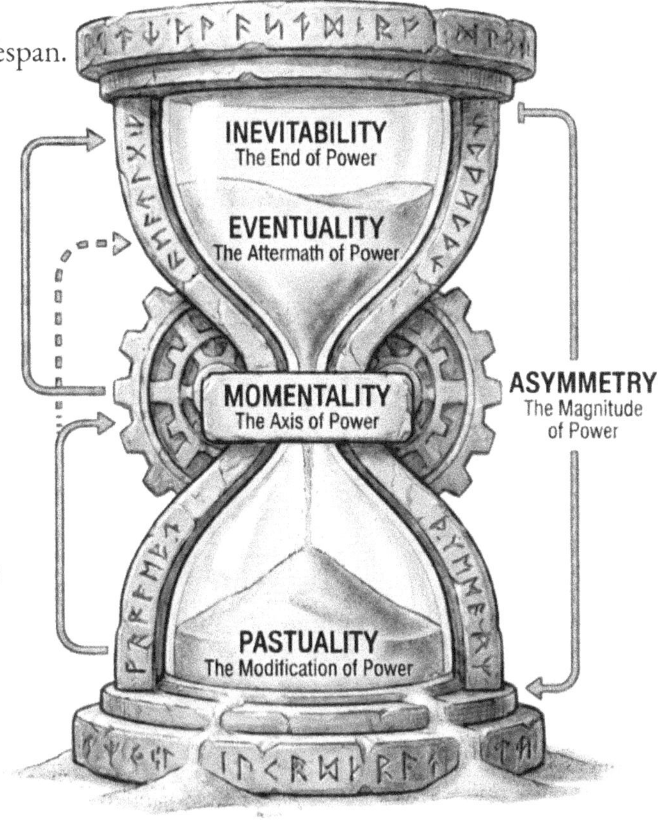

THE "ASYMMETRIC" DECISION
Asymmetry defines your life. The two biggest asymmetric events in my life were 1) A motorcycle accident which delivered lifelong pain and 2) Starting a business which delivered lifelong financial security. What are the two biggest asymmetric events that currently define your life? Note the ease at which you can define them.

Positive Asymmetric Decision: _______________________________________

Negative Asymmetric Decision: ______________________________________

Chapter 2
The Armory of Decision Weapons

Can a few sheets of paper completely change your life for the best, while insuring against the worst? Yep, consider this your lifelong decision arsenal. But context is everything. When your laptop freezes and hits you with the spinning Beach Ball of Death, you don't reach for a claw hammer. And while a calculator might help split the assets in a divorce, no mathematical formula on earth is going to salvage a toxic marriage.

To win the Shadow War, you don't just need weapons—you need the right weapon for the specific enemy. Deploying the wrong tool is just as fatal as deploying no tool at all.

Below is your complete decision armory. I've stripped down all 60+ decision strategies into a rapid-fire briefing, detailing exactly what they do and when to pull the trigger. Each weapon is tagged with its corresponding page number from *Choose Hard, Live Easy* so you can dig back into the primary intel when you need the deep dive. Read and revisit this list often. Sear these concepts into your memory banks until they become as reflexive as breathing. Master the armory, conquer the Moment, and live Easy.

THE ARMORY

- **$600 Pizza Test** – 293: Used to test financial decisions and returns on per unit calculations. Are you paying $600 for a pizza?
- **1/2/3 Divorce Defense** – 257: Use to test your relationship strength before committing to a marriage that could end in a costly divorce, and a costly Eventuality.
- **3As** – Used to war game a process, to continually improve and achieve a great outcome, while steeling motivation.
- **90 Day War Game (Defensive)** – 137: An extrapolation of a process where you repeat the decision at least 90 times, assessing the result after 90 instances. Ex: I ate 90 days of breakfast donuts.
- **90 Day War Game (Offensive)** – 137: A commitment to a process where you invest at least 90 sessions, practices, or instances into a new skill or endeavor. Ex: 90 videos uploaded.
- **Ad Blitz Razor** — 279: The presumption that excessive advertising usually masks an inferior product or service. The company must constantly buy new customers to replace the ones who refuse to return. No one recommends them.
- **Atomic Domino** – 314: The identification of a "to do" variable that makes all other "to do" items less daunting, and more achievable.
- **Attrition Doctrine** – 166: The Awareness and expectations that war is attrition. Expect casualties. In decisions, that is failure, mistakes, and things going sideways.
- **Backcasting** – 217: The deliberate process of reverse-engineering a big goal backward, making goals granular from the distant goal (10 or 5 years) down to weekly and daily goals.

THE ARMORY, CONTINUED...

- **Bayesian Thinking** – 306: The mental process of assigning a confidence score (%) to a likely or unlikely truth, then readjusting the score based on new information.
- **Big Ugly Funeral** – 63: Taking a tragic or sabotage memory and hosting a funeral to end its memory and its hold on you.
- **Buridan Butt Kick** – 282: To overcome struggles with indecision.
- **Business in a Box Razor** – 277: The likelihood that a guru who sells "a business in a box" makes a lot more money selling the idea of the business, than the business itself.
- **Canary Questions** – 250: Poignant questions that are non-confrontational, yet reveal critical decision intel.
- **Death is in the Details** – 243: The notion that critical details in a decision exist, but are buried in complexity or trivial minutiae. UNBLIND the "Blindside" – (Understand, Buried, Lazy, Incomplete, Neglected Detail.)
- **DeMarco's Razor** – 277: Given a choice between two options, the harder option is likely better, provided it meets Responsibility in the Hard Choice Flywheel.
- **Demosthenes** – 175: The process of upskilling and honing talent: A) Shift Expectations B) Deconstruct Target C) Set Small SMG Skirmshes D) Reframe Pastuality E) Attack Weaknesses
- **Directional Probability** – 183: The decisive act of boosting probability FOR or AGAINST you, hence, manipulating luck and their outcomes. Ex: Driving drunk boosts the odds of bad outcomes.
- **Do or Die** – 170: The concept of compelling courage or discipline: If you HAD to do it, or die, would you?
- **Due Diligence** – 239: The act of basic information seeking. Better data = a better choice.
- **Edgelording** – 269: Unleash the internet troll on your decision, effectively red-teaming your choice, revealing the worst or cringiest aspect.
- **Embrace the Suck** – 151: The cognitive Awareness to "embrace the suck" as part of the process and to receive extraordinary outcomes. Greatness is the dividend of many "sucks".
- **Eventuality: Live in Its Skin** – 64: The cognitive Awareness to forecast a decision or a habit into a future you must endure as a state of existence.
- **Expected Value** – 295: Mathematical triage on a financial decision using subjective values and potential outcomes, extrapolated under the premise the decision is repeated thousands of times.
- **FICK** – 143: Fear Is Courage Knocking: Use fear as a "flag" to signal that courage is required.
- **First Principles** – 254: Burning everything to the ground and exposing the root motives or principles the underlie a process, or a decision.
- **Force Multiplier** – 79: Assigning mathematical returns to our decisions. Instead of getting an ROI for our dollars, we discover the punishment or reward on our future moments.

THE ARMORY, CONTINUED...

- **Funk Buster** – 271: A tool to fire gratitude and happiness, instantly shifting perspective.
- **Futurecasting** – 290: A decision time machine which hands habits and decisions to Eventuality, removing the decision from Momentality.
- **Genchi Genbutsu** – 252: Visit the battlefield and get a first hand perspective of the issue, product, or problem.
- **Gratitude Goggles** – 149: A trigger that instantly fires gratitude.
- **Grounding Analogy** – 166: A analogy for a familiar process that is assigned to an unfamiliar process, designed to shift expectations into the right frame.
- **Hack the Kitchen** – 142: Environmental modifications to enforce discipline and make decisions easier through friction or inconvenience.
- **Hansei** – 267: Owning your bullshit and past mistakes, so they don't distort or influence Momentality or Eventuality.
- **Headline Razor**: An ethics test: If what you were doing in private would make headlines, would you be embarrassed and need to post a groveling apology?
- **I am Who I Need to Be** – 172: The Awareness that talent is earned and you can be whomever you need to be in the moment.
- **Identity Anchors** – 138: The adoption of an identity that fosters growth and good decisions.
- **Is This Asymmetrical?** – 300: The simple question that explores the potential of upside or downside asymmetry, even at low odds (<1%).
- **Juggling a Zero (DARE)** – 78: The concept that Nuclear Treason, or DARES, are like juggling zeroes. Good decisions add. Nuclear Treason multiples by zero, instantly eradicating years of good decisions.
- **Kaizen Chess** – 223: The daily decision game involving marginal improvement among the Royal Guard of Happiness. The objective is personal compounding, being better today, than you were yesterday. You are your sole competition.
- **Life As** – 215, 229: The metaphorical lens of reframing life as a video game, a movie, or as the CEO of a company. Through those metaphors, better decisions are made.
- **Luck's Fortune / Death Decks** – 177: The poignant reality that some decisions influence luck. Decisions that boost odds negatively for bad outcomes are draws from the Death Deck, while boosting odds positively is a draw from the Fortune Deck.
- **Maestro Visualization** – 150: A visualization strategy to imbue discipline and discomfort where you picture yourself as a master of the skill you're training for.
- **Memory Alley** – 140: The Awareness and perspective shift to revisit old memories that reflect "how far you've come" and the battle scars you've conquered.
- **Metaphorical Lensing** – 280: The cognitive practice of framing a decision in a metaphorical equivalent that is more familiar.
- **Momentality Detox** – 317: A process to remove waste, overburden, and inconsistency from your life, retaking precious hours.

THE ARMORY, CONTINUED...

- **Monkey First** – 312: A problem solving technique involving identification of a bottleneck, or the primary obstacle in a longer process.
- **North Star Offensive** – 102: A life's purpose or meaning that guides all decision-making, to the effect of amplifying discipline, tolerating discomfort, and firing courage.
- **Pain is Intel** – 150: A feedback signal that growth is underway.
- **Phone Booth Persona** – 129: A shadow operative that "takes no shit" who you can summon in times of needed courage.
- **Pivot and Point** – 132: A visualization strategy where you picture the outcome before executing.
- **Poison Candy Gambit** – 185: A probability tool to evaluate catastrophic risk. You wouldn't blindly eat from a candy bowl if you knew three pieces would kill you instantly.
- **RADAR** – 61: A tactic to reframe a sabotage past; (R)eveal the Big Ugly Moment (A)udit the Story (D)isprove the Story (A)djust the Story (R)epeat.
- **Regret Rehearsal** – 130: Mental time travel where you ask yourself to feel the regret of a decision in the future.
- **Revenue Razor** – 277: When faced with impressive revenue numbers instead of bottom line profits, presume the profit is unimpressive, or worse, negative.
- **Rumsfeld Matrix** – 247: A decision strategy that seeks to uncover critical Unknowns in a decision that will make a decision clearer.
- **Sellout Razor** – 278: The presumption of corporate decline following an acquisition. When a great company is bought out, their loyalty flips from serving you to appeasing Wall Street, triggering a countdown to a garbage product, margin squeeze, and reduced value.
- **SCIRE** – 274: Latin for "to discern or understand," SCIRE is a framework to solve complex problems. (S)ituation (C)auses (I)mpediments (R)ules and Response (E)xecute
- **Silva Codebreaking** – 288: Leveraging your consciousnesses to solve problems during a near-sleep state.
- **Slow the Moment** – 50: The art of recognizing Momentality and the decision you're about to make. Is it Treason? Power? Neutral? Flow?
- **Small Skirmishes** – 132: Conquer fear by engaging in small battles that weaken the fear. If you fear public speaking, you might stand at the next meeting and give a suggestion for 30 seconds.
- **Smallest Min Gain (SMG)** – 141: The strategy of turning a big goal into its smallest minimal gain to imbue motivation and fire a feedback loop. The big goal of saving $1M is reduced to saving pennies.
- **Standing Orders** – 139: A series of laws that are commandments for life, used to enforce discipline and execute Campaign Decisions. "I never check email after 6pm."
- **Stoic Surrender** – 285: The art of surrendering to the flow of life, regardless of preferences, often interpreted as "God's plan" the universe, or serendipity.
- **Stop, Drop, and Roll** – 122: The process to make decisions rationally, void of emotion. Stop and don't decide. Drop and let the emotion subside for 48 hours or longer. Roll with the decision.

- **Talk Some Sense to Him – 68:** Time travel based on *Shawshank Redemption's* Red who wanted to "take some sense" to his younger self. Feel the wrath of the poor decisions "Future You" must suffer and have "Present You" talk some sense to present you.
- **Talk to the Shadow – 136:** *Decision* is Latin for "to cut out." Every decision carries another decision, a shadow transaction. When you make a decision, recognize the shadow and what you are turning down. Working late = "No" to your kid's baseball game.
- **Ten Turns – 143:** Enforce discipline and discomfort through a kickstart of momentum. After 10 minutes, (600 seconds, 60 moments) momentum usually takes over, and you complete the process or session.
- **The Gun + $10M Question – 104:** The cognitive trick that exposes our bullshit. If a gun was put to your head, or if you would receive $10M to DO X, or STOP Y, would you? You would. The strategy highlights that our reasons for DOING X, or STOPPING Y, are simply not strong or prioritized enough.
- **Theaters of War, Intel – 107:** The act of learning, upskilling, or being knowledgeable about your surroundings. These decisions are strategic and should support power, but often are action-faked in the Theater if Chaos
- **Theaters of War, Power – 107:** The only place where decision power can impact your life. These are decisions materially influence your life.
- **Theaters of War, Chaos – 107:** The only place where decision power is wasted, having zero impact on your life. These decisions are like wasting ammo.
- **Then What? – 131:** Part of Worst-Casing, "Then What" asks you to deliberate on the next decision AFTER the worst case occurs.
- **Thinking Razors – 277:** Shortcuts to deciphering ambiguity.
- **Tombstone Razor – 278:** Would this matter if I were dead in 1 year?
- **Trigger Strategy – 144:** Cinching discipline to a trigger. If X happens, you do Y. Rain? You write.
- **Truth Translations – 260:** The art of giving a decision a raw, first principled, translated truth. "Do I want a cigarette" translates to "Do I want a seat at the lung cancer roulette table?"
- **WADM – 302:** The weighted average decision matrix triages several decisions through a subjective analysis of values and factors weighted by their importance. Those are values are summed to arrive at a definitive decision based on a numerical value. Ex: Move = 300, Stay = 220
- **Willpower Bootcamp – 99:** The 12 day bootcamp for exercising willpower, the fundamental muscle of Awareness and Origin of Power.
- **Worst Case WARP Analysis – 121:** Examining a decision and reflecting on the "worst case" outcome, including asymmetry and probability movement.
- **WWJD – 129:** What Would Jesus Do? A tool that borrows the courage or mentality of your favorite mentor or hero, asking, What would they decide in this moment?
- **YODO – 74:** You only die once—the Awareness that death is one moment; the painful path to your death can entail millions of moments.
- **Zero-Based Thinking – 171:** A tool for overcoming sunk cost momentum: Knowing what you know now, would you start fresh on this project or endeavor?

Chapter 3
Decision Gauntlet

ONE MOMENT, ONE LIFE

It only takes 10 seconds to deploy a decision weapon to change your decision, and a potential outcome. Consider the following decision scenarios. For each, I identify the right tool for the situation, followed by the Hard Choice. Note: Multiple decisions weapons can apply.

GHOST PEPPER: As a joke, your co-worker has been eating your refrigerated snacks in the employee break-room. In retaliation, you have acquired some potent ghost pepper sauce. You're thinking about secretly spiking his burrito. What do you do?

Decision Tool to Apply?____

Why?____

What's the Hard Choice?____

NO WIN: You're late for work and you've already been disciplined for tardiness to the point of potential termination. Your driving your child to school who is crying about a project that is due today. He left it at home, and it will severely impact his grades if he gets a zero, ending his straight A track record. What do you do?

Decision Tool to Apply?____

Why?____

What's the Hard Choice?____

THE FLIRTY NEIGHBOR: You're happily married with 3 kids. You are a neighborhood barbecue hosted at the neighborhood clubhouse. While exiting the bathroom, your neighbors' wife starts flirting with you and propositions you a quick sexual encounter. She's drop dead gorgeous. What do you do?

Decision Tool to Apply?____

Why?____

What's the Hard Choice?____

"""

THE DODGY INVESTOR: You have a great business that has been profitable, but need investment money to scale larger and into the realms of life change. You're offered investment money from a person who appears successful, but might be engaged in underhanded/shady dealings. You're desperate. Scale could mean the difference between profiting $100K and profiting $1,000,000. What do you do?

Decision Tool to Apply?____

Why?____

What's the Hard Choice? ____

THE DEDICATED HIKER: You live in Phoenix Arizona and it's May 15th. You're going for a hike up Camelback Mountain at 1pm. It's currently a temperate 93 degrees and dry. You head up the mountain to start your 4 hour hike, and realize within the first few minutes you realize you forgot your water jug. What do you do?

Decision Tool to Apply?____

Why?____

What's the Hard Choice?____

THE BENEVOLENT PARENTS: Your business is booming. But your wife's business is booming even bigger. She's an influencer and makes $20K for every plug on her YouTube channel. You have money to buy your 17 year old teenage son his first car. Due to your unpopular high school trauma, you want to buy him a Corvette which will rocket his popularity. Your wife wants to buy him a Toyota Tacoma truck. What do you do?

Decision Tool to Apply?____

Why?____

What's the Hard Choice?____

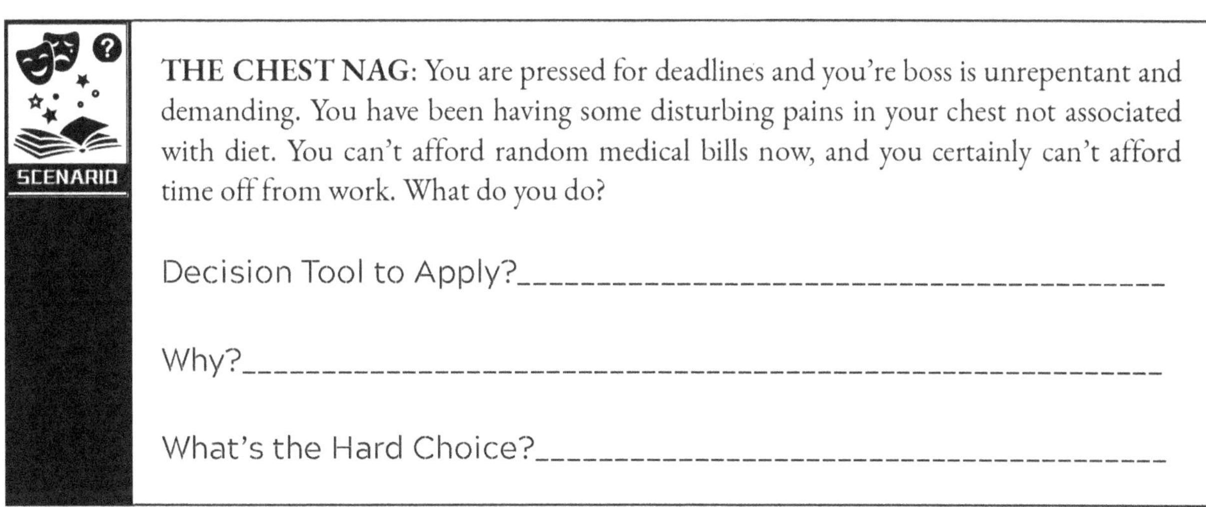

THE BLAST FROM THE PAST: You're happily married. An old high school girlfriend contacts you and wants to reconnect. You do, exchanging casual banter, but she continues to call and wants to FaceTime daily to share emotional support. You're wife is secure, trusts you, and doesn't perceive this ex as a threat. What do you do?

Decision Tool to Apply?____

Why?____

What's the Hard Choice?____

THE CHEST NAG: You are pressed for deadlines and you're boss is unrepentant and demanding. You have been having some disturbing pains in your chest not associated with diet. You can't afford random medical bills now, and you certainly can't afford time off from work. What do you do?

Decision Tool to Apply?____

Why?____

What's the Hard Choice?____

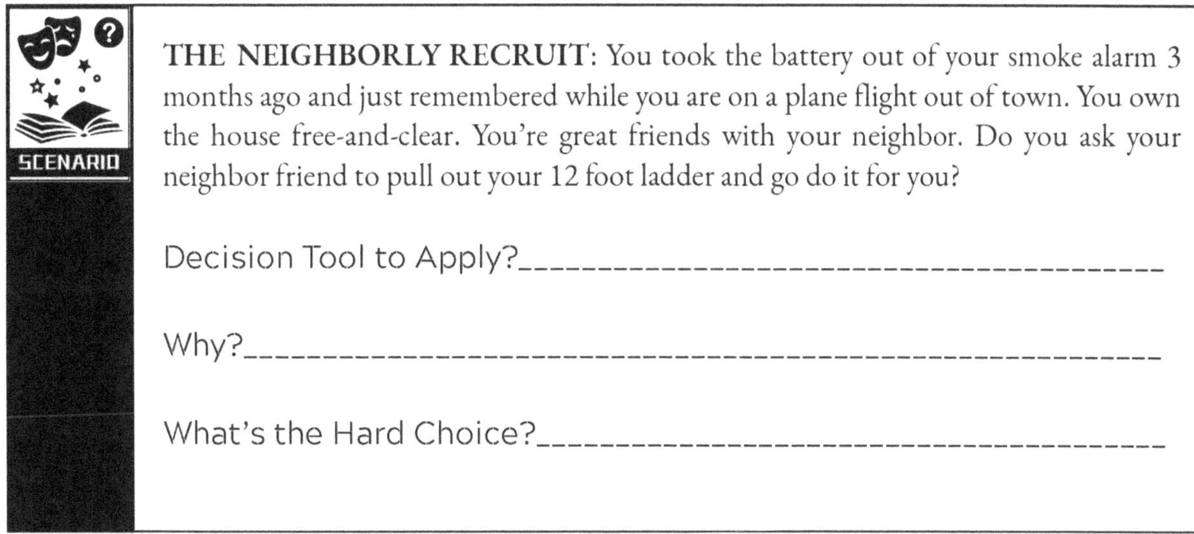

THE NEIGHBORLY RECRUIT: You took the battery out of your smoke alarm 3 months ago and just remembered while you are on a plane flight out of town. You own the house free-and-clear. You're great friends with your neighbor. Do you ask your neighbor friend to pull out your 12 foot ladder and go do it for you?

Decision Tool to Apply?____

Why?____

What's the Hard Choice?____

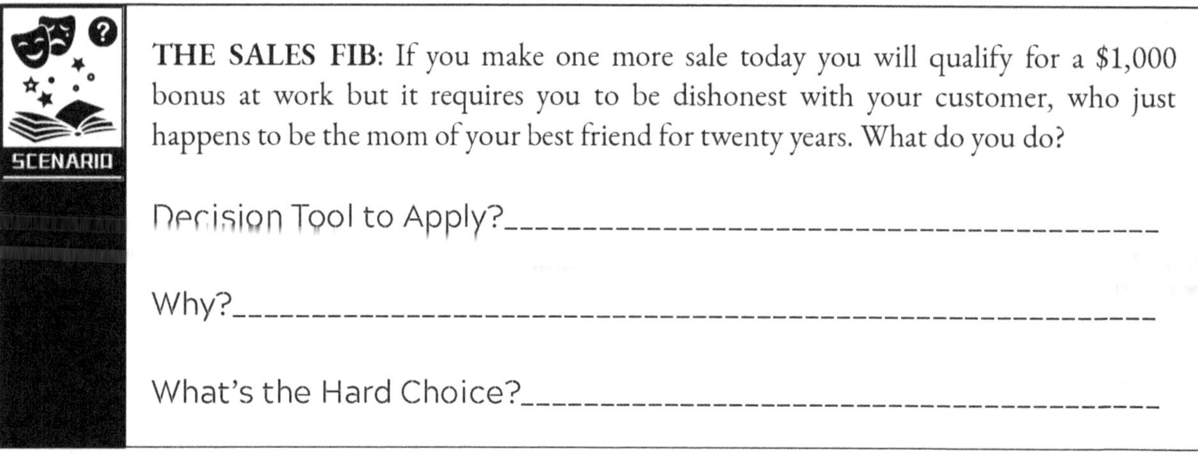

THE SALES FIB: If you make one more sale today you will qualify for a $1,000 bonus at work but it requires you to be dishonest with your customer, who just happens to be the mom of your best friend for twenty years. What do you do?

Decision Tool to Apply?____

Why?____

What's the Hard Choice?____

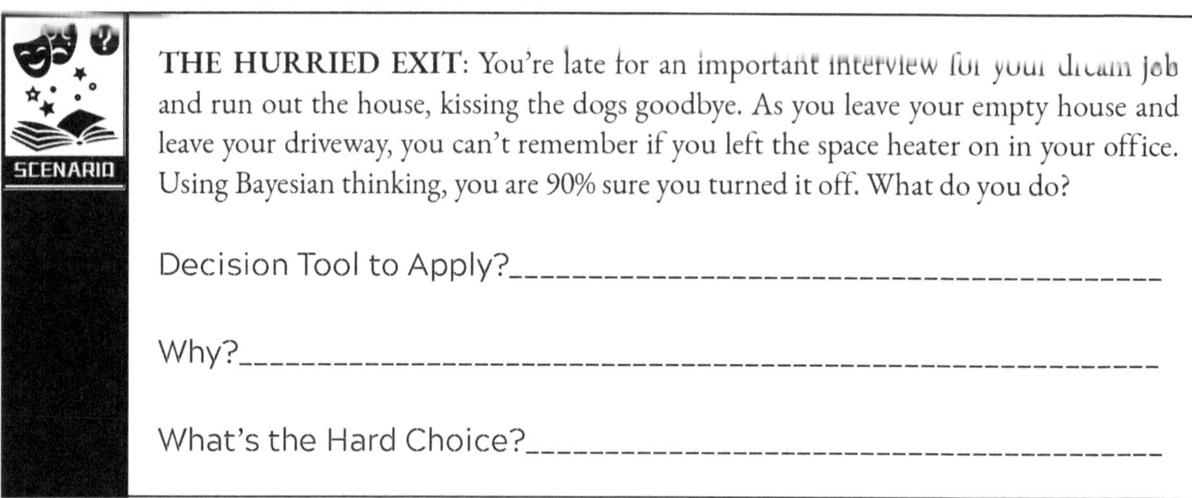

THE HURRIED EXIT: You're late for an important interview for your dream job and run out the house, kissing the dogs goodbye. As you leave your empty house and leave your driveway, you can't remember if you left the space heater on in your office. Using Bayesian thinking, you are 90% sure you turned it off. What do you do?

Decision Tool to Apply?____

Why?____

What's the Hard Choice?____

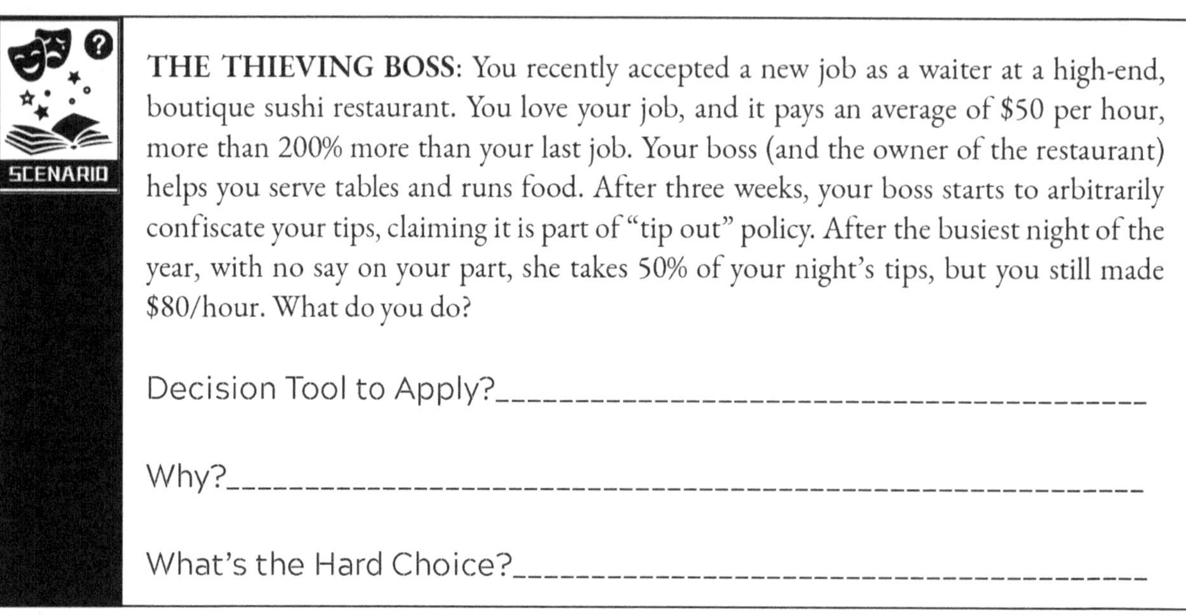

THE THIEVING BOSS: You recently accepted a new job as a waiter at a high-end, boutique sushi restaurant. You love your job, and it pays an average of $50 per hour, more than 200% more than your last job. Your boss (and the owner of the restaurant) helps you serve tables and runs food. After three weeks, your boss starts to arbitrarily confiscate your tips, claiming it is part of "tip out" policy. After the busiest night of the year, with no say on your part, she takes 50% of your night's tips, but you still made $80/hour. What do you do?

Decision Tool to Apply?____

Why?____

What's the Hard Choice?____

THE OLD FRIENDS: You haven't had a drop of alcohol for months as you understand it is poison. Your friends invite you to a night out and they all drink, often getting rowdy and rambunctious, making you feel like an odd person out. Do you go knowing that alcohol isn't aligned with your goals? Or do you blow off your friends, again, for the 10th time? What do you do?

Decision Tool to Apply?______________________________________

Why?______________________________________

What's the Hard Choice?______________________________________

THE SLOTHFUL SPOUSE: You've recently changed your perspective on health and longevity. You're tired of being tired. You're tired of medications, aches, and pains. You start exercising and change your diet. You've lost 30 lbs, feel great, but the momentum is starting to dwindle. Your spouse isn't on board, doesn't support you, and fills the kitchen with junk food. A divergence is occurring. What do you do?

Decision Tool to Apply?______________________________________

Why?______________________________________

What's the Hard Choice?______________________________________

THE FOOD SUBSCRIPTION: Constant fatigue and job stress leads you to pick up drive through fast food on the way home from work. Shopping, cooking, and cleaning takes up a lot of time and energy, resources you feel you don't have. You are considering a meal service that will deliver healthy meals to your door. It is super expensive and will strain your budget to its limit, forcing you to make cuts elsewhere. What do you do?

Decision Tool to Apply?______________________________________

Why?______________________________________

What's the Hard Choice?______________________________________

THE FRONT: You have an important job interview coming up and need to look your best. Unfortunately, you can't afford a new outfit and you're behind on some credit card payments, but you need to look the part for the potential job. Do you buy the outfit that you can't afford? Or do you risk looking like you don't belong? Or is there another solution? What do you do?

Decision Tool to Apply?____

Why?____

What's the Hard Choice?____

THE DOG ATTACK: You're in your home and hear a ruckus outside. You look out the window of your house and witness a woman and her poodles are being attacked by violent bulldog. The woman and her dogs are screaming in terror. What do you do?

Decision Tool to Apply?____

Why?____

What's the Hard Choice?____

THE PROPOSAL: You've been dating someone for 3 months who wants to get married. They're on a work visa and have captivated your heart and soul. If you don't get married, they will return home to their native country, leaving you heartbroken. What do you do?

Decision Tool to Apply?____

Why?____

What's the Hard Choice?____

OUTCOME: THE DECISION GAUNTLET

Make a decision for both the Flirty Neighbor and the Benevolent Parents. Roll your dice for each, and turn to the back of the workbook (Dice Appendix) to see potential outcomes for your decision.

Chapter 4
The Invisible Witness

THE SHADOW WAR

You are currently engaged in a covert conflict known as The Shadow War. Unlike traditional warfare fought with tanks and missiles, this war is fought with economics, dopamine, and cultural engineering. The battlefield is not a plot of land; it is your mind, your attention span, your wallet, your vitality, and your nervous system.

DECISION COMBAT: THE EASY/HARD PARADOX

The fundamental law governing the Shadow War is the Easy/Hard Paradox. It is the ancient duality that determines how you will live—or suffer—through your life.

The default nature of combat paradox is Easy, an invisible alliance which operates in the margins of comfort, convenience, and apathy. The system is megalithic, omnipresent, and neuro-manipulative. From the social media platforms that addict you to a vortex of scrolling to the sugar-spiked food you eat, the system thrives on plausible deniability. The system seduces you into self-destruction as anxiety, disease, depression, and misery are profitable. A demon guild of hardship awaits.

THE TRAP: When you choose EASY (comfort, avoidance, instant gratification), you are punished with HARDSHIP (poor health, poverty, anxiety, regret).

THE ESCAPE: When you choose HARD (responsibility, courage, discipline, discomfort), you are rewarded with EASE (freedom, vitality, wealth, peace).

THE COMMANDER'S AWARENESS

Your real life begins the moment you stop blaming your absent parents, bad luck, or your poor genetics, and acknowledge the war. You are not cursed or a victim; you are under covert attack. Recognize the propaganda for what it is. Acknowledge that every time you swipe, sip, or splurge on autopilot, you are becoming a prisoner of war. The only way to win is to stop saying YES to Easy, and NO to a system that wants you sick, indebted, and unhappy.

THE INVISIBLE WITNESS

For the last 168 hours (7 days), I, MJ DeMarco, have been a ghost in your life. I watched you from dusk to dawn. I sat in your passenger seat. I looked over your shoulder at your phone screen. Yep, even while you sat on the toilet. I watched what you put in your grocery cart and in your mouth. I watched how you spent your free time. No moment was missed, including how you behaved when no one was looking.

PART 1: THE CURRENT REALITY

How would I rate the current reality of your life based on the video footage? Rate from 1 - 10.

- 1 = Disaster/Pathetic
- 5 = OK/Survival
- 10 = Elite/Mastery

MJ's RATING: MY REALITY

What did I witness? Remember this number for a dice challenge at the end of this module.

THE RATING: ___________________

THE RULES:
I have no investment in your feelings. I know nothing about your potential. I did not hear your dreams, your excuses, your plans, or your prayers. I only witnessed your physical actions, or inactions. Based solely on that footage, I am submitting my report and observations to you.

FINANCIAL REALITY

Observation: What did I see you buy? Did you save or invest? Did you produce value or just consume it?

MJ's RATING: FINANCIAL

What did I witness financially?

THE RATING: ________________

CAREER TRAJECTORY

Observation: Did I see deep work and skill acquisition, or quiet-quitting posts on Reddit? Did I see meaning and purpose?

MJ's RATING: PURPOSE

What did I witness about your work?

THE RATING: ________________

SPIRITUAL HEALTH

Observation: Did I see peace and gratitude? Or anxiety, doom-scrolling, and dopamine addiction?

MJ's RATING: SPIRITUALITY

What did I witness spirituality?

THE RATING: ________________

RELATIONSHIPS

Observation: Did I see presence and connection? Or distracted nodding while looking at a phone?

MJ's RATING: YOUR TEAM

How is the team surrounding you?

THE RATING: ________________

PHYSICAL HEALTH

Observation: Did I see sweat and natural food, or sofas, sugar, and drive-thru double-cheeseburgers?

MJ's RATING: YOUR HEALTH

What did I witness financially?

THE RATING: ________________

PART 2: THE FUTURECAST (Rate 1 - 10)

Futurecasting is your Time Machine, revealing how decisions compound later and projecting the consequences into a brutal Eventuality you can't ignore.

Behavior × Repetition = Eventuality

You won't die from a single soda, cigar, or missed workout. But these choices don't act alone. They combine with others, each with its own potential impact. You're shaping your future, brick by brick, bite by bite. Before the 10,000th time, there was the first time.

I am feeding the last week's footage into a predictive algorithm. Assuming you change NOTHING and assuming this week is your normal, your permanent operating system— where are you in 5 years?

FINANCIAL REALITY
- 1 - Broke / Dependent
- 5 - Surviving
- 10 - Financially Secure

MY FINANCIAL FORECAST
Where are you headed financially?

THE RATING: _________________

CAREER TRAJECTORY
- 1 - Dead-end shit jobs
- 5 - Tolerant career
- 10 - Fulfilling career

MY CAREER FORECAST
What is your career

THE RATING: _________________

SPIRITUAL HEALTH
- 1 - Depressed/Apathetic
- 5 - Just OK
- 10 - Joyful, alive, grateful

MY SPIRIT FORECAST
What did I witness spirituality?

THE RATING: _________________

RELATIONSHIPS
- 1 - Alone and lonely
- 5 - Few good people
- 10 - Rich relationships

YOUR TEAM FORECAST
How is the team surrounding you?

THE RATING: _________________

PHYSICAL HEALTH
- 1 - Diseased, Medicated
- 5 - Surviving
- 10 - Healthy, top 5% for age

YOUR HEALTH FORECAST
What did I witness financially?

THE RATING: _________________

PART 3: THE DEFENSE
You vehemently disagree with the report above. You scream, "MJ! That's not who I am!" You claim I missed the real you. I retort, "Sorry, your actions reflect your priorities, not your intentions."

THE EVIDENCE:
You're in a court of law and your own defense attorney. List the specific evidence that proves the video footage as wrong. Since I witnessed every action, most of what is here must be an intention, a wish, or a thought. Write them down, and realize that all intentions are worthless if they never translate into behavior. Reading a book is not going to impress the judge; applying it in the real world does. Did I see that?

MY EVIDENCE AND DEFENSE

____

____

____

____

____

____

PART 4: THE RESHOOT

I am coming back in 1 month and once again will be ghost filming you for a week. What specifically will appear on the footage next month that was missing this week for each element in the Royal Guard of Happiness? (Do not write "I will try harder." Write the specific action I will see.)

MY PIVOTS

FINANCES:____

____

CAREER:____

____

SPIRITUALITY:____

____

RELATIONSHIPS:____

____

MY HEALTH:____

____

Everybody wants to change their life, but few people want to change their choices. And ultimately, this changes nothing. This Futrurecasting exercise demonstrates what is waiting for you in your Eventuality, a reality you must endure.

Your Axis of Power and ability to change your life rests in the moment of decision. Change something, or change nothing. The future is yet to be written.

OUTCOME: THE INVISIBLE WITNESS

Remember your "Current Reality" assessment from Part 1, the rating I would give you? Remember it, roll the dice, and turn to the back of the workbook (Dice Appendix) to see potential outcomes for your future, the skin you are sewing.

Chapter 5
Your DEFCON (Decisional Fallout Condition)

The military uses DEFCON to measure war readiness. Your personal DEFCON measures your Decisional Fallout Condition, an unvarnished snapshot of how secure or screwed up your life currently is based on your past choices. Are you operating from a fortified baseline of peace (DEFCON 5), or are you spiraling toward the total annihilation of DEFCON 1

To determine your current threat level, answer the following 25 questions with ruthless honesty. There is no gray area here: if your answer isn't a crystal-clear "Yes," it is a hard "No." Do not negotiate with your ego or perform mental gymnastics to protect your feelings. Bullshitting yourself is an Easy casualty; facing your actual baseline is Choosing Hard and your first victory. If you performed this exercise in the main book, repeat the test and see if it has improved or worsened.

QUESTION	YES	NO
1) Do you need to lose more than 20 lbs of excess body fat?		
2) Is more than half the food you eat processed? Hint: Fruits, vegetables, seeds, nuts, legumes, fish, and lean meats are not processed.		
3) If your 10-year-old self saw you today, would they be disappointed in the life you lead and uninspired by what you've accepted?		
4) Are you currently taking prescription meds to manage lifestyle-driven conditions?		
5) Do you have any legal addictions: sugar, caffeine, nicotine, gambling, social media, porn, alcohol, weed, or gaming? Hint: Every day is an addiction.		
6) Do you carry a credit card balance month to month?		
7) If your income vanished for three months, would your life spiral into chaos?		
8) Is your retirement fund zero, or a plan based on "someday," an inheritance, or a utopian fantasy?		
9) Is your net worth negative?		
10) Is your credit score under 700?		
11) Have you lost more than $1,000 gambling on crypto, meme stocks, or sports bets in the past 3 months?		
12) Do you lack two close friends with whom you can be fully honest at any time?		
13) Do you have a pattern of staying in loveless, unsupportive, or strained relationships long after you know they're over?		
14) Is your primary method of resolving conflict to "win" the argument?		

QUESTION	YES	NO
15) If you had an unscheduled, quiet hour with no phone or computer, would you feel intense boredom or anxiety?		
16) Do you lack inner peace and struggle with anxiety, depression, or nihilism?		
17) Do you regularly consume outrage-focused media (political news, culture war commentary, etc.) that leaves you feeling angry or fearful?		
18) When you make a mistake or fail, is your first instinct to blame external factors or other people?		
19) Is your self-worth tied to the car you drive, the designer clothes you wear, or social media validation?		
20) Are you afraid of what others think or say about you?		
21) Do you suffer from the Sunday Blues—dread for the coming workweek?		
22) Do you spend more than seven hours a week consuming passive entertainment like sporting events, video games, or social media?		
23) Have you gone a whole month without doing four things that frightened or challenged you?		
24) Has it been over a year since you intentionally learned a new skill outside of work or school?		
25) Do your wildest dreams feel dead, unrealistic, or unreachable, especially within the next 5–10 years?		

CALCULATING YOUR DEFCON SCORE

Answer YES or NO to all 25 questions. Each YES is a precision strike from Easy in your territory, while a NO is a solid defense.

- **<u>STEP 1</u>**: Total your NO answers.
- **<u>STEP 2</u>**: Multiply by 4. (That's your score out of 100.)

Formula: ([Sum: NO answers] × 4) = Your DEFCON DFS Score
Example: 20 "NO" = 80 Defcon Score

DFS SCORE	DEFCON LEVEL	INTERPRETATION
96,100	5	Wow. You're a powerful bad-ass winning the Shadow War through domination. Easy doesn't have a chance.
92	5	You're dialed in. Your best self is running the show, and fear is often conquered. Easy rarely runs through your veins.
88	4	You're ahead of most, but there's some room for improvement, as you are not operating at full Power.
80,84	4	Decent. You're consistent, and Hard is overpowering Easy. But more work is needed as Easy co-opts command occasionally.
76	3	You're doing OK. But OK is where Easy gains strength, and weakness gains power.
72	3	You're walking the thin line. Some days you choose Hard, but most days you don't. Easy is the dominant drug, claiming territory.
68	2	Danger zone. You're not failing, but you're operating with a severe power deficiency. Wake up soon, or be conquered.
60,64	2	You're bleeding out in the trenches. Easy has the high ground. Power drained. Annihilation is imminent.
Under 60	1	Easy owns your ass. You've surrendered all power. You're a drug-addicted prisoner of war. Social media awaits your tirade.

OUTCOME: YOUR DEFCON SCORE

Your DEFCON is a reflective accumulation of your choices and the consequences they have wrought. Assuming you CHANGE NOTHING and continue on your current path, roll your dice and remember the number. Turn to the Dice Appendix and look up your likely future.

I gave this test to several artificial intelligence systems and asked what the average person would score based on available data. The results were dismal: 16, 20, and 24.

Chapter 6
Your Decisional Situation Report (SITREP)

Most people refuse to take ownership of their lives. They love a scapegoat. They blame their emotionally absent parents, the economy, AI disruption, or their ninth-grade math teacher rather than the person staring back in the mirror. Your DEFCON score gave you the surface threat level, but your Decisional SITREP is the advanced autopsy.

Think of the SITREP as a blood test for your decision-making life. The numbers do not lie. This diagnostic combines the unfiltered truth of how you feel with the cold, hard facts of how you actually live. It strips away the excuses and reveals exactly where your resources are bleeding out.

Are you a Pessimistic Losing Pawn, or an Optimistic Winning General? It's time to calculate your Decisional SITREP. Do not fudge the numbers. Bullshitting yourself is an Easy casualty; telling the truth is a Hard win.

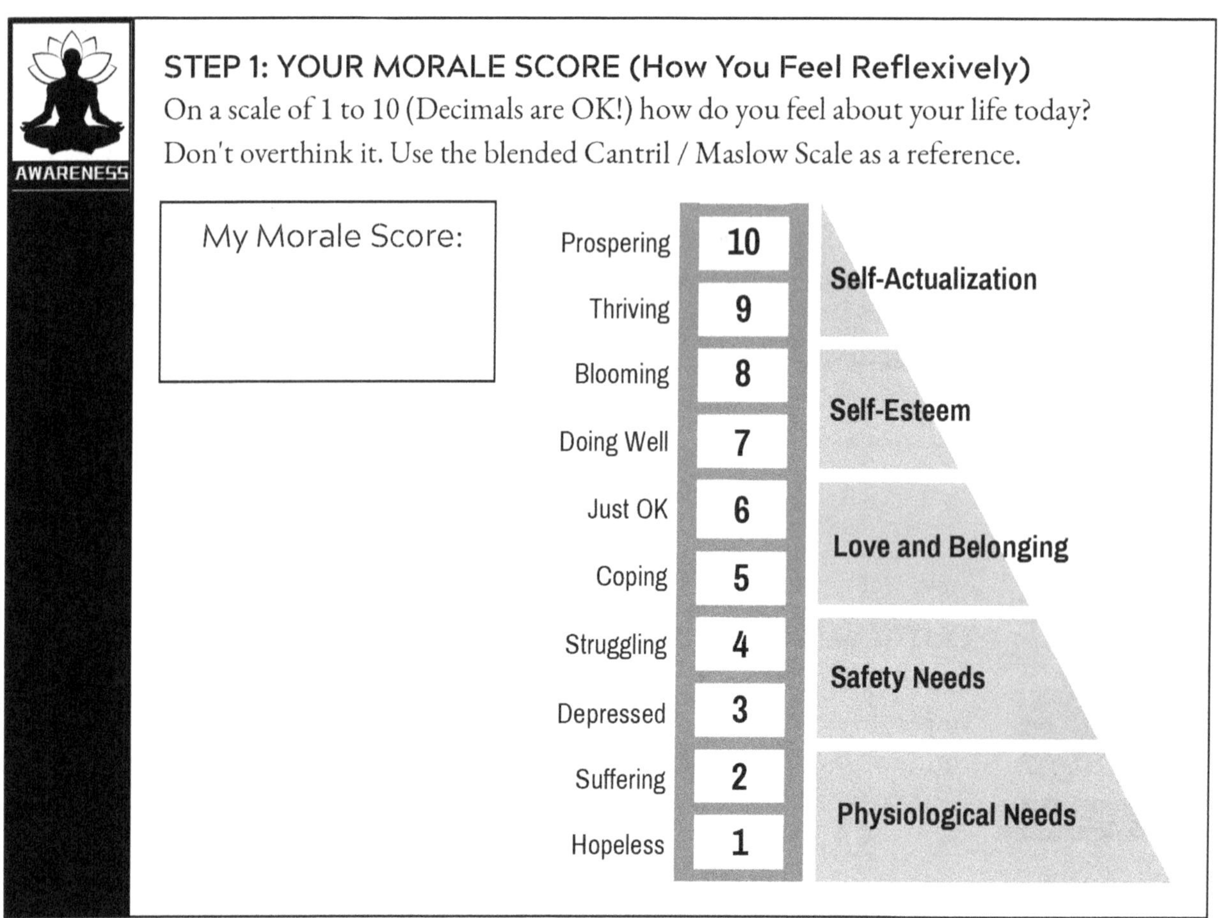

STEP 2: THE ROYAL GUARD OF HAPPINESS (The Facts)

Now, rate the five critical pillars of your actual life on a scale of 1 to 10. These factors are essential pillars of happiness based on countless studies. Multiply your rating by the assigned weight to get your true Combat Score for each.

HEALTH (The King):

Energy, vitality, absence of disease, weakness, pain.

Rating: _________ x 1.2 = [___________]

FREEDOM (The Queen):

Financial autonomy, ability to control of your time, optionality.

Rating: _________ x 1.1 = [___________]

RELATIONSHIPS (The Rooks):

Deep connections, friends in your foxhole, spouse.

Rating: _________ x 1.0 = [___________]

SPIRITUALITY (The Bishop):

Connection to something greater, peace, reverence for life.

Rating: _________ x 0.9 = [___________]

PURPOSE (The Knight):

Meaningful work, impact, a reason to wake up on Monday.

Rating: _________ x 0.8 = [___________]

STEP 3: YOUR COMBAT COMMAND SCORE

Add your 5 scores together, then divide by 5 to find your factual foundation.

Total Score: _________ ÷ 5 = [Command Score: _________]

STEP 4: YOUR COMMAND RANK

Locate your Command Score on the scale below to find your official rank.

- (9.5 - 10) Commander
- (9 - 9.4) General
- (8.5 - 8.9) Colonel
- (8 - 8.4) Lieutenant
- (7 - 7.9) Sergeant
- (6 - 6.9) Soldier
- (5 - 5.9) Conscript
- (3 - 4.9) Pawn
- (2 - 2.9) Hostage
- (1 - 1.9) Prisoner
- (0 - 0.9) Zombie

My Command Rank: _______________________________

STEP 5: THE AXIS OF AWARENESS (Your Waystone Gravity)

This measures the chasm between the life you have and the story you tell yourself about it. Are you Slowing the Moment, or are you crippled by the ghosts of Eventuality and Pastuality? Subtract Command Score from Morale Score.

<u>The Formula:</u>
Morale Score:_______-Command Score:_______=Morale Gap:________

THE VERDICT:

- Positive Number = OPTIMISTIC and a premium on joy. Your Waystone lifts you. You operate with gratitude and resilience. (A +1.1 = 110% premium!)
- Negative Number = PESSIMISTIC. Your Waystone drags you down. You are paying an anxiety tax on a life that is objectively better than you think it is. A -.80 is an 80% tax on happiness.

My Waystone Gravity
☐ Optimistic ☐ Pessimistic   %
Premium/Penalty

STEP 6: THE AXIS OF MOMENTUM (Your Victory/Defeat Index)

Are you conquering territory or losing it? For the next 24 hours, audit every choice you make. Every action (or avoided action) is a bullet fired. Run each choice through the 90-Day War Game: If I repeat this for 90 days, does my life get better or turn to shit?

THE SCORING KEY:

- +2 = Double Power (e.g., Treadmill + Audiobook)
- +1 = Power Choice (e.g., Healthy lunch, writing a chapter)
- 0 = Neutral Flow (e.g., Getting dressed)
- -1 = Treasonous Choice (e.g., TikTok binge, skipping gym)
- -2 = Double Treason (e.g., DoorDash pizza + 4 hours of video games)
- -10 = Nuclear Treason (e.g., Driving drunk, cheating on your spouse)

MY DAILY DECISION PORTFOLIO

> _____________________Pts___ > _____________________Pts_____
> _____________________Pts___ > _____________________Pts_____
> _____________________Pts___ > _____________________Pts_____
> _____________________Pts___ > _____________________Pts_____
> _____________________Pts___ > _____________________Pts_____
> _____________________Pts___ > _____________________Pts_____
> _____________________Pts___ > _____________________Pts_____
> _____________________Pts___ > _____________________Pts_____
> _____________________Pts___ > _____________________Pts_____
> _____________________Pts___ > _____________________Pts_____
> _____________________Pts___ > _____________________Pts_____
> _____________________Pts___ > _____________________Pts_____
> _____________________Pts___ > _____________________Pts_____
> _____________________Pts___ > _____________________Pts_____

TOTAL: ________   TOTAL: ________

YOUR 24-HOUR V/D INDEX TALLY:

Add up your total Power points and subtract your Treason points.

- Positive Total = **WINNING**. You are on the offensive.
- Negative Total = **LOSING**. You are in full retreat, begging the Brekkians for another hit.

My Victory/Defeat Index

[ ] Winning   [ ] Losing

STEP 7: YOUR DECISIONAL SITUATION REPORT (SITREP)

Combine your three intel points to set your current battlefield identity. This is your badge of honor, or dishonor.

[Waystone Gravity] + [Victory/Defeat Index] + [Command Rank]

MY DECISIONAL SITREP

I am an [_____________], [_____________] [_____________].

Example: "Optimistic, Winning General" or "Pessimistic, Losing Pawn."

Chapter 7
The Pastor in the Parking Lot

It's late afternoon. You are in the seediest part of town, waiting for your lawnmower at a repair shop. Across the street sits "Going Googoo for Girls," a notorious strip club rumored to skirt the edge of the county's indecency laws.

As you sit in your car, the door to the club opens. You freeze. Walking out, looking hurried and keeping his head down, is your church's Youth Pastor. Shocked, you instinctively pull out your phone and record a video. It's grainy, but it's definitely him and he's adjusting his belt buckle. He gets in his car and speeds off.

You go home and show your wife. She's mortified but feels vindicated—she always said he gave her a creep vibe. She wants to post the video to social media immediately to "protect the community."

The Dilemma: The Easy choice is to post it and punish the duplicitous creep. It feels righteous. It feels like justice. But is it? The Hard choice is to pause, suppress the outrage, Slow the Moment, and run the decision protocols.

DRILL #1: CODE OF CONDUCT
Does a youth pastor visiting a strip club violate your Code of Conduct?

☐ YES ☐ NO ☐ MAYBE ☐ NOT MY BUSINESS

BAYESIAN THINKING
Bayesian Thinking is the art of thinking in probabilities about situations where information is missing, murky, or unclear. It starts with a "base rate"— the likelihood of X being true. As new information (Unknowns) are exposed and become clear, you change your probability.

DRILL #2: BAYESIAN THINKING
Based on the known information A) The Pastor was at strip club B) Your wife always had creep vibes and C) The pastor was fastening his belt buckle as he left, what percentage of probability do you give that the Pastor is involved in sordid activities and the creep your wife suggested?

My % "Base Rate" that the pastor is involved in un-Pastorly activity. ☐ %

DRILL #3: RUMSFELD UNKNOWNS

What is a Unknown Known in this scenario? What information is out there that is missing, and would give absolute clarity to everything?

UNKNOWN KNOWN ____

DRILL #4: THE 5 LAWS ANALYSIS

Before you let your wife hit "Post," run the decision through the 5 Laws of Decision Power.

1. MOMENTALITY

Are you acting on temporary emotion or permanent logic?

____

2. EVENTUALITY

If you post this, what is the domino effect of consequences for his family and yours?

____

3. ASYMMETRY

What is the Upside vs. the Downside? Do you gain anything? What do you lose if you're wrong?

____

4. INEVITABILITY

In the context of your death, does "exposing" this man matter? Is this how you want to spend your limited time?

____

5. PASTUALITY

Looking back in 10 years, will this memory bring you pride or justice (*We kept the church pious!*) or regret and cruelty *(That didn't end well!)*?

____

DRILL #5: THE BAYESIAN CONFIDENCE TRACKER

You are now an investigator. Examine the Bayesian % you assigned in Drill #2. You encourage your wife to Stop, Drop, and Roll before posting the video. She agrees to wait 48 hours. During that time, you decide to gather more intel. Consider each of these scenarios, independent of each other

SCENARIO A: You call the Pastor's wife and ask a "Canary Question" ("How is [Husband]? I haven't seen him."). She replies: "Oh, he's been running around all day counseling distressed parishioners."

Does this change your confidence? What is your new %? ☐ %

SCENARIO B: You call a friend who knows the area. You learn that several young women from the community have fallen on hard times and work at that specific club.

Does this change your confidence? What is your new %? ☐ %

SCENARIO C: After a couple of phone calls with friends, you discover the Pastor also runs a side hustle as a plumber.

Does this change your confidence? What is your new %? ☐ %

SCENARIO D: You visit the Pastor. You ask him point-blank. He shows you a text from a father begging him to go to the club and drag his runaway daughter out.

Does this change your confidence? What is your new %? ☐ %

SCENARIO A,B,C, and D: All of the above are true.

Does this change your confidence? What is your new %? ☐ %

OUTCOME: THE PASTOR IN THE PARKING LOT

Roll your dice and turn to the back of the workbook (Dice Appendix) to see potential outcomes for this decision and how they play out in the future.

Chapter 8
The Benevolent Burglars

Bill is troubled. He's pouting about the dilemma he faces.

"Every night, my home is robbed," Bill explains. "The burglars steal money, jewelry, and irreplaceable valuables. Some of these things I will never get back. Never."

Tears fill his eyes.

Jim looks at him, horrified. "OMG, that's a nightmare! Have you called the police? Do they smash the windows or bust down the door with a ram?"

Bill shakes his head. "No, I won't call the police. And I insist on leaving the doors unlocked."

Jim, utterly confused, asks, "I don't get the problem. Why don't you just lock your freaking doors? Better yet, lock them and install a security system. Do something and stop these robbers from stealing your precious stuff!"

"Well, that's my thing," Bill says, looking away sheepishly. "I don't want to lock my doors, and I certainly don't want to install any security."

Jim looks dumbfounded, his mouth hangs open.

Bill continues, "You see, the burglars always leave me a plate of chocolate chip cookies. And they are the most delicious cookies I've ever tasted. In fact, I think there might be some type of narcotic baked into them because I simply can't get enough of them. They are so good that now I leave my doors unlocked every minute of every day."

Bill picks up one of the cookies and takes a bite, his eyes rolling back into his head in satisfaction. "And now I'm going broke." He chews the last of his cookie and continues. "The problem is, I know these burglars are robbing my life blind, but I can't seem to find the motivation to lock my doors."

Jim stares at him. "So not only are you getting robbed, you're being drugged?"

"Yes," Bill whispers.

"And you continue to allow it?"

Bill looks at the empty space where his life used to be. "Yes."

THE "CHOOSE HARD" REALITY: YOUR SCREEN STEALS MOMENTALITY

This isn't a story about burglars, jewelry, or a house—it's a story about the glowing box in your pocket that whispers in your ear every minute of the day. Your smartphone is the open door. The algorithm is the burglar. And all those notifications you refuse to silence? Those are the narcotic-laced cookies.

Every "like," every "ping," and every "infinite scroll" is a carefully engineered bribe designed to keep you sedated while Big Tech pillages your most irreplaceable asset. Your attention. Your precious, irreplaceable time. They are stealing your focus, your ambition, and your presence with your family, and they are doing it in broad daylight. And if you're like Bill, you are complicit in the theft, refusing to make the Hard choice.

<u>BREAKING NEWS:</u> You aren't "staying informed" or "staying connected." You are being processed. Monetized. You are trading your time (and a potential legacy) for a digital sugar high that might as well be a narcotic. If this doesn't freaking piss you off and inspire action—sorry—nothing will.

HIJACKED AWARENESS
When your Awareness is Hijacked, so is your Power.

The origin of your Power is Awareness.
If you don't command your Awareness, you don't command your energy.
If you don't command your energy, you don't command your decisions.
If you don't command your decisions, you don't command your Power.

THE DRILLS

Open your phone. Go to Settings > Screen Time (or Digital WellBeing on Android).

DRILL #1: THE GROSS NUMBER

Write down your Daily Average. If you play video games via computer/console (and the accurate number is not reflected from your phone data) add your daily playtime.

MY DAILY AVERAGE OF SCREEN TIME...

______________ HOURS   ____________ MINUTES

This number represents the total time you spent staring at a screen yesterday.

DRILL #2: SUBTRACT TOOLS AND NECESSITIES

Yep, context matters. Some of your screen usage was pure Tool usage (Maps, Work, Uber). Some of it was Toy usage (Scroll, Swipe, Envy).

ADD THE FILTER: TOOLS VERSUS TOY

Tap "See All App Activity." Review the list. Subtract any time spent on Power/Power Flow activities (e.g., Maps, Texting Spouse, Uber, Spotify for Gym, Audible for Learning). These are Tools. Everything else (Social Media, News, Games, Shopping) is Hijacked Awareness. These are Toys.

DRILL #3: THE NET HIJACK

Calculate your True Hijack number (Gross Number minus Tools).

MY DAILY HIJACKED AWARENESS...

______________ HOURS   ____________ MINUTES

This number is the total time your Awareness was hijacked and stolen.

MISUSED WEAPONRY POINTED IN YOUR FACE
How you use your phone is your choice.
You can use it as a weapon of mass instruction.
Or as a weapon of mass destruction.

Choose Hard: your screen is a powerful weapon working for "Best You".
Choose Easy: your screen is a bong, a syringe, or worse, a gun pointed in your face.

THE COMMANDER'S STANDARD

To show you the difference between a Tool and a Toy, here is my personal audit for a day.

MJ's DAILY AVERAGE FOR SCREEN TIME

______**3**______ HOURS ______**38**______ MINUTES

I spend an average of 3 hours and 38 hours using my phone daily.

<u>The Context</u>

- Spotify: 2 hours (Gym/Writing Soundtrack) — POWER FLOW
- Audible: 1 hour (Walking Dog/Sleep) — POWER FLOW
- Maps/Texting: 29 minutes + (Logistics) — NEUTRAL

MY DAILY HIJACKED AWARENESS...

______**0**______ HOURS ______**9**______ MINUTES

This number is the total time my Awareness was hijacked and stolen.

My Net Hijacked Awareness: 9 minutes.

DRILL #4: THE COMPOUNDING ASYMMETRY OF STUPIDITY

Take your Daily Hijack number from Step 3 and multiply it by 7.

MY <u>WEEKLY</u> HIJACKED AWARENESS...

______________ HOURS ______________ MINUTES

This number is the weekly hours of Awareness hijacked and stolen.

DRILL #5: FACE THE HARD REALITY

If your number is 8 hours, you deleted one full workday from your week. If your number is 16 hours, you deleted more than one full month of 8-hour workdays from your year. Look at that number again. Imagine if you spent that time investing in "Future You," like building a business, fixing your body, or connecting with your kids.

DRILL #6: THE EXECUTION ORDER–MAKE THE HARD CHOICE

Identify the #1 Toy app/game/time suck responsible for your Hijacked Awareness.

THE LARGEST THIEF OF MY AWARENESS

The App or Game ____

MAKE A HARD CHOICE

☐ I will delete the app/game/or toy.

☐ I will create a Standing Order.

THE ORDER ____

I don't use social media unless it is relevant to my business. I can't do X, unless I do Y.

VICTORY!   **DEFEAT!**

Victory = I deleted the app. Defeat = I didn't delete the app, or action-faked and gave the app a time limit.

DRILL #7: THE REALLOCATION

You just found X hours of free time per week. You are going to reinvest this capital into a Campaign Commitment. (Do not pick a passive hobby like "watching movies.")

Pick an active skill, goal, or an investment in your Eventuality: Woodworking, sewing, coding, copywriting, guitar, Brazilian Jiu-Jitsu, lose 100 lbs, learn to snowboard, starting a YouTube Channel—something that will advance your life in any facet of the Royal Guard of Happiness.

If you could snap your fingers and possess Top 10% proficiency in one skill, what would it be? Don't worry about time or your current set of skills.

I WILL INVEST MY RECLAIMED AWARENESS INTO...

The Skill or Hobby____

Replace the screen time with something that is an investment in "Future You".

8) THE CONTRACT

Don't lie to yourself. Promise yourself. Commit to the Campaign Decision and sign a contract to reclaim your power.

Step 1: Ditch the primary thief of Awareness.
Step 2: Make the commitment to replace the liability with an asset.
Step 3: Sign the contract

My Contract & Commitment for Reclaimed Power and Awareness

I, _______________________________, on this date _______________________________,
[Your name]

refuse to leave my doors unlocked and remain complicit in the theft of my life's

most precious resource, time. In endeavor to reclaim my Awareness, my time, and

my Power, I agree to lock the doors to my most egregious offender of theft

_______________________________ and rechannel and refocus that Awareness
[Name the application/burglar]

into _______________________________ as an investment in "Future Me"
[Name the new skill or talent]

who must bear the skin I am currently sewing.

Sign Here: ____

THE THREE THEATERS OF WAR

Decisions and their power to influence your life is like shooting a weapon. Is that weapon aimed at a specific target? Or are you firing it into the ground, wasting precious ammunition? Most people waste their lives and their decision Power in the Theater of Chaos.

THE DISTRIBUTION OF POWER

<u>THE THEATER OF POWER</u>: The Zone of Control.

This is where decision impacts your life. It is direct action, like pulling a lever and moving probability. Your best life is built in the Theater of Power.

<u>THE THEATER OF INTELLIGENCE</u>: The Zone of Strategy.

This is planning, learning, and observing. Intelligence supports Power, but often times, it is abused in into action-faking. Reading 50 books on business is Intelligence. But it only becomes Power when that intel is passed into the Theater of Power.

<u>THE THEATER OF CHAOS</u>: The Zone of the Uncontrollable.

Decisions here are worthless. They can't change your life positively, only negatively. This is the land of a Hijacked Awareness. This is politics, the news, mindless YouTube shorts, other people's opinions, the weather, and the past. This is where your worst life is built, fought on hills that don't matter, and can't be won.

HIJACKED AWARENESS = THEATER OF CHAOS

Calculate the percentage of time you spend weekly in Chaos. Divide your weekly total minutes (Drill #4) by 5040 (total waking hours 12 hours or 720 minutes) to find your total.

Chaos = Weekly Hijacked Awareness Minutes / 5040

This is the (%) of resources are wasted in the Theater of Chaos with a Hijacked Awareness.

MJ'S CALCULATION .... **1.25 %**
9 Daily Minutes X 7 = 63 weekly minutes / 5040

YOUR CALCULATION .... **%**

DRILL: SKETCH YOUR BATTLEFIELD

In the space on the next page, draw the Three Theaters of War that best represents your average day. Draw proportional circles and assign 3 percentages (%) that add up to 100%. Start with the CHAOS % listed above. Think about your last 48 hours of decision power and how it was allocated. I've included my personal sketch.

- <u>CHAOS</u>: How much time did you spend angry at the news? Arguing with idiots about pro sports teams? Fighting digital zombies? Worrying about uncontrollable shit that doesn't matter?
- <u>INTEL</u>: How much time did you spend learning? Researching? Upskilling? Planning? (Intelligence)
- <u>POWER</u>: How much time did you spend executing? (Power)

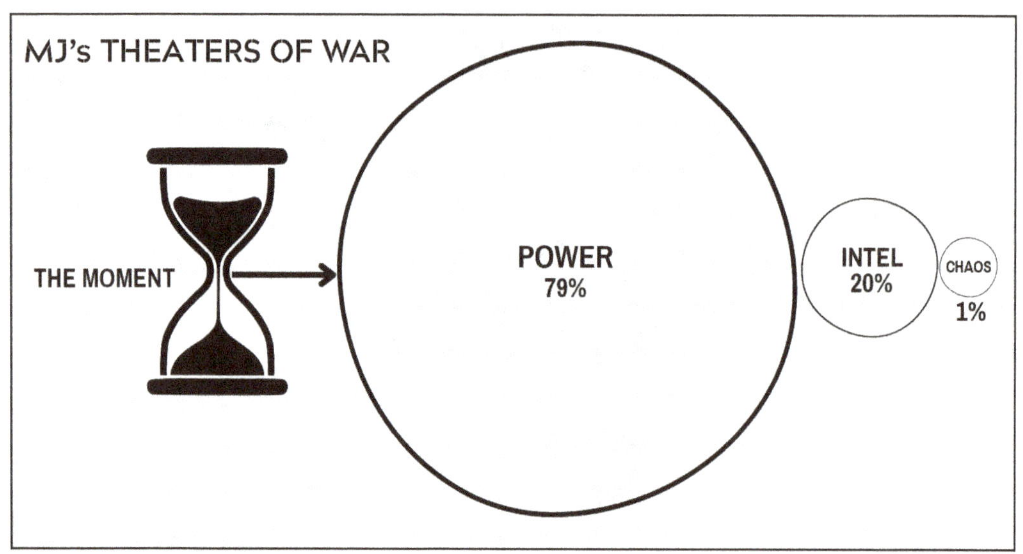

YOUR THEATERS OF WAR

THE DEBRIEF

Examine your sketch. Here's how a life optimized for Power and success should look.

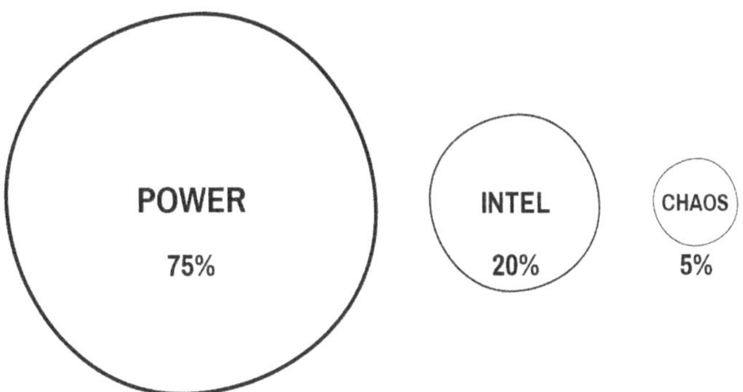

If Chaos is larger or the same size as Power or Intelligence, you are bleeding out in the trenches of the Shadow War. You are a soldier standing in the middle of a battlefield shouting at the sky and flailing your arms, instead of digging a foxhole and aiming your ammo (Power).

THE ADDITIONAL CHAOS EVICTION:

Within your Contract for Reclaimed Power you already eliminated a Chaos hijacker. Now, Identify another source of Chaos you will ditch immediately and replace with either Power or Intelligence. (Ex: "I will stop reading political comments on Twitter and instead learn how to play piano.")

THE EVICTION:____

ITS REPLACEMENT: ____

Identify one shift from Intelligence to Power. (Ex: I will stop reading about X, and start doing X!_

Chapter 9
The Unwritten Future

THE SCENARIO:
Right now, you are a traveler standing at a crossroads. Two alternate futures exist simultaneously. The intelligence is out there:

- Your DEFCON (60 or less?)
- Your SITREP (Losing, pessimistic, and a command rank soldier or less?)
- Your weekly Hijacked Awareness (Greater than 12 hours?)
- Your wasted Power in The Theater of Chaos (Greater than 20%?)

All of these are brutal indicators which version is winning. Is it Worst You, or Best You? Both are real possibilities. One is built by Hard Choices. The other is from Easy Choices. You do not stumble into these futures. You write them, one decision, one Momentality at a time. And right now, your metrics are becoming a skin you will wear.

PART 1: THE COMMANDER (The "Best You")
Visualization: Fast forward 10 years. You made the Hard Choices, took responsibility, faced the discomfort, and stayed disciplined. You corrected your DEFCON, SITREP, and Chaos issues. The compounding asymmetry of Hard has paid off, and your Royal Guard of Happiness is in a state of Command. Describe this reality using the prompts below:

THE KING: The Health/Body:
How's your energy? What do you see in the mirror? Muscles? Be detailed!

THE QUEEN: Your Freedom and Optionality

Net worth? Passive income? Toys? Emergency fund? Can quit your job? Move?

THE BISHOP: Spirituality/Mental Health

How is your spiritual life and your connection with life? Mental health?

THE KNIGHT: Purpose/Meaning/Career:

What kind of work you doing? Your mission? Your North Star Offensive?

THE ROOK: Your Relationships / Human Connection

Who is beside you? What is the quality of your connections?

THE LIFESTYLE + THE EASE

Where do you live? What do you drive? How do you spend Tuesday? Describe the Ease that your Hard has been rewarded.

THE CONSTRUCTION PLAN

To build this "Best You" reality, what are the Three Campaign Decisions* you must commit to, starting today? A Campaign Decision is a commitment to a new habit or lifestyle. Here are some examples:

Operation 100: My commitment for longevity and the goal of living as a centenarian.
Operation Financial Freedom: A commitment to financial security.
Operation Debt Free: Pay off debt
Operation Start a Business: Become an entrepreneur

 CAMPAIGN DECISION #1

CAMPAIGN DECISION #2

CAMPAIGN DECISION #3

DISCIPLINE: STANDING ORDERS

A Standing Order is a steadfast rule you adopt to enforce discipline. A Standing Order is like a law that you cannot break, except the law is not a societal law, but a personal life law. For example: "I don't eat after 6pm" is a Standing Order. For each element in the Royal Guard of Happiness, create 1 or 2 Standing Orders.

STANDING ORDERS: HEALTH
What Standing Orders will help you live out your best health?

ORDER #1:____

ORDER #2:____

STANDING ORDERS: FREEDOM / FINANCES
What Standing Orders will help you live out your best financial life?

ORDER #1:____

ORDER #2:____

STANDING ORDERS: SPIRITUALITY
What Standing Orders will help you live out a peaceful, spiritual life?

ORDER #1:____

ORDER #2:____

STANDING ORDERS: MEANING/PURPOSE/CAREER
What Standing Orders will help you give your best purpose and fulfillment?

ORDER #1:____

ORDER #2:____

STANDING ORDERS: RELATIONSHIPS
What Standing Orders will help you create the strongest relationships?

ORDER #1:____

ORDER #2:____

PART 2: THE PRISONER OF THE SHADOW WAR (The "Worst You")

Fast forward 10 years. You chose Easy. You binged Twitch and Netflix. You bought the toys on credit. You ate the garbage and scrolled like a zombie. You avoided Hard like the black plague. You are now a Prisoner of the Shadow War. Write the misery and feel it.

THE KING: The Health/Body:

What do you see in the mirror? Obesity? Meds? Arthritis? Your knees? Sleep?

THE QUEEN: The Freedom/Wealth:

Are you living paycheck to paycheck? Working late? Suffocating in debt and stress?

THE BISHOP: Your Spirit & Mental Health

Are you depressed? Apathetic? Lost in a digital void?

THE KNIGHT: Purpose/Meaning:

What's your job? Are you waking up at 5AM doing meaningless work you hate?

THE ROOK: Your Relationships / Human Connection

Who is beside you? Are you lonely and without intimate connection?

THE HELLPSAN + THE HARDSHIP

Describe your horrible living conditions. Describe the clunker car you drive, or the bus you need to ride. End with one word or phrase that describes your worst life.

----------------------------------- ONE WORD:_____________________

THE REGRET REHEARSAL (ANTI-GOALS):

The Regret Rehearsal is psychological time travel. It vividly applies the Inversion mental model, famously advocated by billionaire investor Charlie Munger. He said, "All I want to know is where I'm going to die, so I'll never go there." Instead of trying to be brilliant, just avoid stupidity. He believed the best way to lead a good life is first to pinpoint everything that would lead to a miserable one.

TIME TRAVEL

Name 6 behaviors, habits, or decisions that would absolutely guarantee that you would lead a miserable life, or the "worst version" of you.

(1)_________________________ (2) _____________________________

(3) ________________________ (4) _____________________________

(5) ________________________ (6) _____________________________

How many of these behaviors, habits, or decisions are you currently engaging in? Hint: It likely relates to Chaos activities, or tiny treasonous choices, such as, "I smoke cigarettes whenever I go to night clubs or raves."

NUMBER OF BEHAVIORS: ____________

THE LICENSE: WHAT WILL TRIGGER THESE BEHAVIORS?

Below is a list of Easy saboteurs that will fight for "Worst You". What specific mental license will allow these behaviors to take hold? In other words, where will you justify lying to yourself? Check any that apply.

☐ The "It tastes good" Easy.	☐ The "You only live once" Easy.
☐ The "I want it now" Easy.	☐ The "I deserve it" Easy.
☐ The "I don't feel like it" Easy.	☐ The "It's been a long day" Easy
☐ The "I'll worry about it later" Easy.	☐ The "I don't have time" Easy.
☐ The "It won't happen to me" Easy.	☐ The "I don't know how" Easy.
☐ The "Everyone's doing it" Easy.	☐ The "I'm not good at that" Easy.

You are writing two short letters to your future self. Be honest, raw, and emotional. And remember, whichever these come true (or any variation) you will endure these moments as a state of existence.

AWARENESS

LETTER A: TO MY "WORST SELF" (10 Years from Now)

Write a letter of Regret to the "Worst You" who choose Easy and didn't do the work. You didn't avoid the anti-goals and engaged in treasonous behavior. Every Easy saboteur ran rampant. Curse them for sewing the skin you're now suffering; the poor diet, the poor habits, the poor planning, the poor job, the poor finances—the poor everything! Be a Red and "Talk some sense to him!"

Dear Future Me,

LETTER B: TO MY "BEST SELF" (10 Years from Now)

Write a letter of gratitude to "Best You" who did the work and avoided the behaviors you listed in the Regret Rehearsal. Thank them for banishing Easy's saboteurs: taking the time to exercise, the sweat, the saving money, the upskilling, and enduring the Hard so they could enjoy the Easy.

Dear Future Me,

____

____

____

____

____

____

____

____

____

____

____

____

____

Chapter 10
Hack the Kitchen

ENVIRONMENT MATTERS

Having the discipline to kill "Worst You" while creating "Best You" isn't just about willpower; it's a battle of terrain. In The Unwritten Future, you just described both scenarios within all five elements of Happiness's Royal Guard.

"Hacking the Kitchen" is the tactical manipulation of your physical environment to force discipline in the moment using friction or inconvenience. You don't need iron-clad willpower if you simply remove the temptation. The premise is powerful but basic: if the trash isn't in your kitchen pantry, you can't eat it at midnight. Modify your perimeter, and you hardwire the Hard choice.

HACK YOUR KITCHEN - THE HAPPINESS ROYAL GUARD

What environmental changes can you make within the 5 happiness factors to enforce discipline and better choices? Don't make statements, make declarations.. "I will X".

HEALTH

What changes can you make to your environment to make better health choices? Yes, this starts in your kitchen, but extends elsewhere. For example, I have better workouts at a public gym surrounded by healthy people, rather than working out alone in my basement.

Change #1: ____

Change #2: ____

Change #3: ____

FREEDOM

What changes can you make to your environment to make better choices for freedom and finances? Cut up credit cards? Avoid malls? Pay cash? Brainstorm.

Change #1: ____

Change #2: ____

Change #3: ____

SPIRITUAL / PEACE / MENTAL HEALTH

What changes can you make to your environment to make better choices for your spirit, peace, and mental health? Volunteering? Ditch outrage porn?

Change #1: ____

Change #2: ____

Change #3: ____

MEANING / PURPOSE / CAREER

What changes can you make to your environment that will help your purpose in life? Your career? Your feeling of fulfillment? Join a club? Mentorship?

Change #1: ____

Change #2: ____

Change #3: ____

RELATIONSHIPS

The people in your orbit are either force multipliers or emotional anchors. That tired cliché about being the average of the five people you associate with? It's a mathematical certainty in the Shadow War. Take a hard look at your inner circle. Who is co-signing your excuses and validating your Easy choices? If your squad is a liability leading you toward the abyss of mediocrity? List the the vampires who you might need to let go.

Person #1:___________________ Person #2:___________________

Person #3:___________________ Person #4: ___________________

A metaphorical lens for the people in your life is like an open door.
Those doors can lead to greatness, growth and happiness.
Or those doors can lead to suffering, stagnation, and misery.
Choose wisely who you allow into your life.

Chapter 11
Backcasted Best Life

INTELLIGENCE BRIEFING: BACKCASTING
You identified the Power draining forces, Chaos and Hijacked Awareness. You just described your best and worst life. You "hacked the kitchen" and changed your environment, Now, we will plan and reverse engineer your wildest dreams, while sidestepping the nightmares.

Most people live their lives piling bricks blindly, unaware of where the road actually leads. Backcasting, or what I refer to as a "1/5/10 Plan," is the antidote to this drift. It is the process of engineering your best life by starting at the finish line—your personal "Everest"—and working backward to the present moment. Unlike a crystal ball that predicts every twist, Backcasting acts as a compass, ensuring that today's decisions are not random, but specific steps moving you toward a defined destination.

The strategy is simple but phenomenally effective: You define an ambitious long-term goal (say in 10 years) and break it down into a triad of milestones—typically 5 years, 1 year, and eventually, weekly objectives. This method transforms insurmountable mountains into actionable molehills. By focusing your power on a single weekly mission, you ensure that your immediate actions are effectively baby steps that bridge the gap between your current reality and your ultimate ambition.

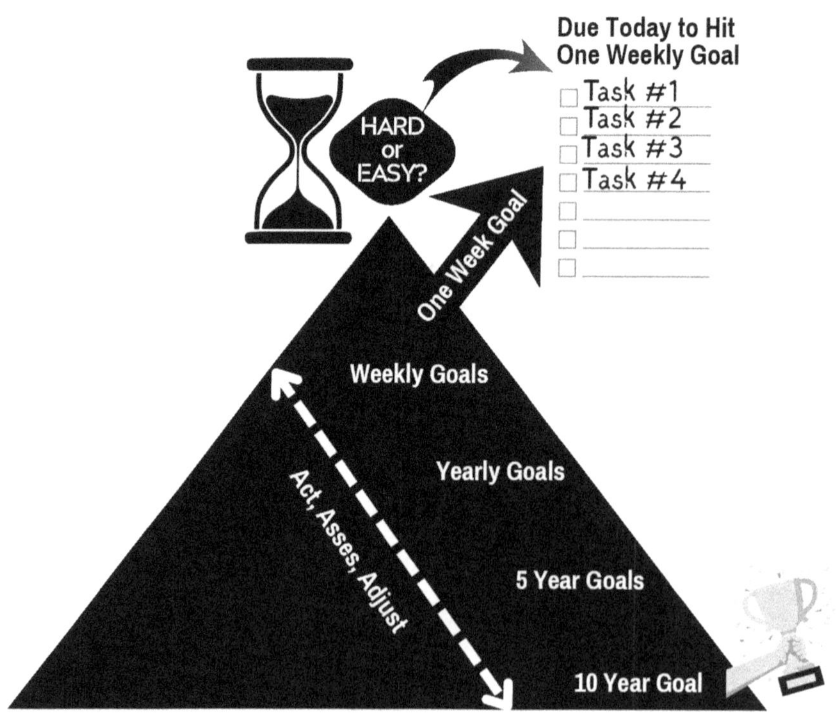

Success is rarely stumbled upon as an *Event*; it is a planned *Process*. While you cannot foresee every detour or pivot, Backcasting demands that you become the architect of your future rather than letting culture build it for you. The magic and the momentum are found in executing the work right in front of you, one week at a time. While you might not land exactly where you wanted, you might land somewhere just as good, if not better.

BACKCAST A CAMPAIGN DECISION

In Chapter 8 (The Benevolent Burglars), you defined (3) Campaign Decisions, long-term commitments to particular goal or outcome. Pick ONE and create a comprehensive Backcasting plan.

Do not get hung up on the math. Whether you use a 10/5/1-year split or a 5/3/1-year split is irrelevant. The increments are merely checkpoints. Their only job is to bridge the gap between impossible and next Tuesday. If the gap between two years feels too wide, add a checkpoint. If it's too small, skip it.

EXAMPLE: OPERATION FINANCIAL FREEDOM

If your goal is to be debt free with $200,000 investable cash within 5 years, your backcast might look like this:

- Year 5: $200,000 liquid. I celebrate.
- Year 3: Side business is cash-flowing $5,000/month; expenses are capped.
- Year 1: First product/service is live with 10 recurring customers. Debt free.
- 6 Months: Product scaling; 50% of debt repaid.
- 1 Month: Product validation, marketing plan drafted. Debt pay off plan drafted.
- 1 Week: Research 5 competitors and identify where I can create value skew.

CAMPAIGN DECISION (THE BIG GOAL!)

In [ ] Years My Goal Is:____

3/5/10 years

Break it Down by Half (What needs to happen to be halfway to the big goal?)

In [ ] Years Goal #1:____

2/3/5 years

Goal #2: ____

Goal #3: ____

Goal #4: ____

Goal #5: ____

Break it Down By Half (What needs to happen to be halfway there?)

In [ ] Years Goal #1: _______________________________________

1/2 years

Yearly Goal #2: _______________________________________

Yearly Goal #3: _______________________________________

Yearly Goal #4: _______________________________________

Yearly Goal #5: _______________________________________

Monthly Goals (What needs to happen to be halfway to yearly goals?)

In [ ] Months Goal #1: _______________________________________

3/6/9 months

Monthly Goal #2: _______________________________________

Monthly Goal #3: _______________________________________

Monthly Goal #4: _______________________________________

Monthly Goal #5: _______________________________________

Weekly Goals (What needs to happen to be halfway to monthly goals?)

In [ ] Weeks Goal #1: _______________________________________

1/2/3 weeks

Weekly Goal #2: _______________________________________

Weekly Goal #3: _______________________________________

Weekly Goal #4: _______________________________________

Weekly Goal #5: _______________________________________

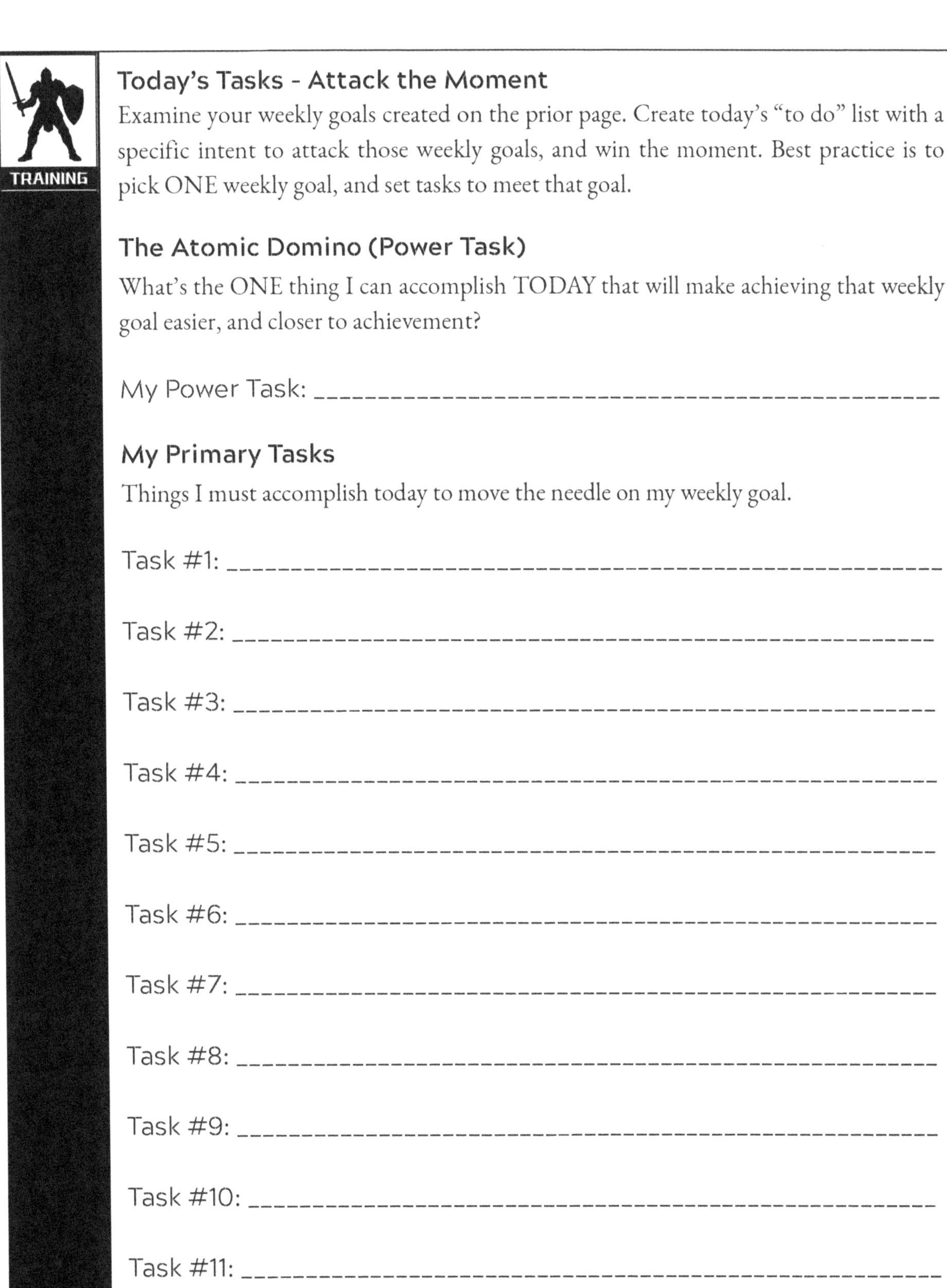

Today's Tasks - Attack the Moment

Examine your weekly goals created on the prior page. Create today's "to do" list with a specific intent to attack those weekly goals, and win the moment. Best practice is to pick ONE weekly goal, and set tasks to meet that goal.

The Atomic Domino (Power Task)

What's the ONE thing I can accomplish TODAY that will make achieving that weekly goal easier, and closer to achievement?

My Power Task: ____

My Primary Tasks

Things I must accomplish today to move the needle on my weekly goal.

Task #1: ____

Task #2: ____

Task #3: ____

Task #4: ____

Task #5: ____

Task #6: ____

Task #7: ____

Task #8: ____

Task #9: ____

Task #10: ____

Task #11: ____

Task #12: ____

In Appendix G, you can find various Backcasting "to do" lists for download and printing.

Chapter 12
XMAS at the Coffee Shop

It is December 22nd. The crowded coffee shop is warm, smelling of peppermint and roasted beans. Michael Bublé is crooning overhead. You are tucked into a cozy corner, finishing the final slides of a career-defining presentation due tomorrow. Your tote bag is on the floor—containing your laptop, your wallet (credit cards/ID), your house keys, and the fob to your new SUV parked outside.

You feel a sudden, violent rumble in your stomach. The coffee has turned on you. Bad creamer? You need a bathroom now or something bad is going to happen, and it won't be pretty. You look to your left. There is a grandmotherly in her 60s knitting a scarf.

SCENARIO #1: You dash to the bathroom, leaving your booth.

SCENARIO #2: You make eye contact with the old lady, smile, and ask, "Ma'am, would you mind watching my stuff? I'll be back in 30 seconds."

She smiles warmly and says, "Of course dear, go." Relieved, you dash to the restroom.

OUTCOME:

Three minutes later, you return. Your stuff is gone. The grandma is gone. Your bag is gone. You run to the window. Your SUV is gone. You reach for your phone to call the police, but you realize it's in the bag, too. In 180 seconds, you will be digitally and physically erased. No ID. No money. No car. No house keys. And your boss's presentation is on a hard drive, currently traveling at 80mph down the interstate.

THE FOUR RULES OF ENGAGEMENT

The Easy decision was leaving your valuables unprotected. The Counterfeit Hard was asking the old lady to be their protector. You risked $80K in assets and oodles of time (Car+Identity+Job) to save a table worth $0. Frame the decision using the 4 rules.

POLARITY

Choosing Easy delivered Hard. What (2) Hard Choices would have secured Easy?

#1:____

#2:____

<u>Hard Choice #1</u>: Taking 15 seconds and the physical effort of unplugging your charger, packing your bag, and carrying it into a dirty bathroom stall

<u>Hard Choice #2</u>: You could have left your coffee and coat (low value) in the booth to symbolize its occupation, but take the bag (High Value) with you.

TRANSIENCE:

How long did the Easy relief last? How much time did it save?

____

____

PERSISTENCE:

How long will the Hard consequences last?
(Identity theft, insurance claims, possible job loss, inconvenience last?)

____

____

IMMINENCE:

How much Hard (Hellpsan) did this invite into your life?

____

____

EXERCISE: LAWS OF DECISION POWER
MOMENTALITY: (The Axis of Power)

Did you treat this moment as trivial? Put yourself in the situation.

In Your Judgment, What Was the Probability of a Bad Outcome?

.1%   1%   5%   10%   20%   33%   50%

EVENTUALITY: (The Aftermath of Power)

List the "Hellspan" dominoes that fall because of this one choice.
Examples: Car stolen -> Can't get home -> Can't open doors > Locksmith >Forward...

(1)_______________________________   (2)_______________________________

(3)_______________________________   (4)_______________________________

(5)_______________________________   (6)_______________________________

PASTUALITY: (The Modification of Power)

Would you decision have changed if the little old lady looked like a famous fraudster you once saw on *Dateline*? Or if another patron in the coffee shop reminded you of a dodgy person?

YES   NO

Without RADAR, how might this traumatic outcome impact future choices?

(1) ____

(2) ____

(3) ____

ASYMMETRY: (The Magnitude of Power)

Define the potential explosive aftermath.

What was the Upside of this Decision? _________________________

What was the Downside? ______________________________________

What was the Force Multiplier? _______________________________

Review the Probability You Circled on Prior Page...

At what probability would you modify your decision calculus and identity the potential asymmetric downside (Dare/Treason) and a draw from life's Death Deck?

.1%   1%   5%   10%   20%   33%   50%

Poison Candy Gambit

I'm offering you $50,000 for the following DARE: You must eat a piece of candy from a bowl. The problem? One piece of candy is laced with cyanide. You'll die painfully in 4 minutes if you pick that candy. Is there any level of odds that would make you reach in the bowl and pick a candy?

| 1 in 1000 | 1 in 500 | 1 in 250 | 1 in 100 | 1 in 50 | 1 in 25 | 1 in 10 | NONE |

Note: If you didn't select "NONE" you are playing from luck's Death Deck. Even 1 in 1000 odds is unacceptable downside.

WEAPON DEPLOYMENT

Reflect on how each decision weapon could have changed your decision at the coffee shop to A) Leave your things unattended or B) Ask the old woman to play protector.

WORST-CASING WARP Analysis.
(Worst Case, Asymmetric Risk, Probability)

Worst Case Outcome? ____

Asymmetric Risk Profile?____

Directional Probability and Movement to Luck's High Ground

What actions could have boosted the probability of a good outcome, giving you luck's high-ground? (Hint: Hack the Kitchen). Remember, a decision that boosts the odds of a bad outcome is a decision from luck's low-ground. And a poor decision.

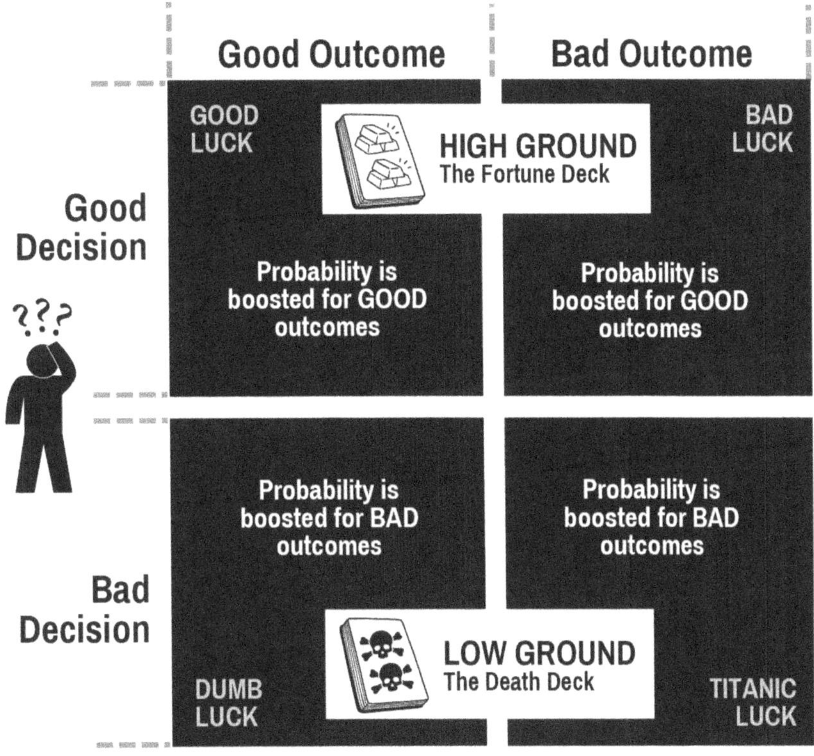

Action #1:____

Action #2:____

WEAPON DEPLOYMENT, CONTINUED

When we're in the middle of making an impulsive decision—like leaving your valuables unprotected at a crowded coffee shop—it only takes one moment (10 seconds) and decision weapon to change the decision, and hence, change the odds and the outcome. The weapon is not important. Changing the decision is.

YOU LIVE IN THE SKIN YOU SEW

Feel the skin you'll endure for the worst outcome.

REGRET REHEARSAL

Feel the regret, stress, and anxiety of the worst outcome

DEATH IS IN THE DETAILS

What details did I possibly not notice about the old woman? Or the crowd?

(1) _______________________________ (2) _______________________________

(3) _______________________________ (4) _______________________________

IS THIS ASYMMETRICAL?

Could these simple 3 words have instantly
stopped the decision to leave your valuables?

YES   NO

RUMSFELD MATRIX

What "Unknowns Knowns" did I miss and hope did not exist?

(1) _______________________________ (2) _______________________________

OUTCOME: XMAS AT THE COFFEE SHOP

It's XMAS at the coffee shop and you've ignored this exercise, leaving your valuables to run to the bathroom. Turn to the back of the workbook (Dice Appendix) to see potential outcomes for this decision future.

Chapter 13
The Uncomfortable Comfort Zone

THE COMFORT ZONE

In Chapter 11, you created a Backcasting Plan that engineered your dream life. As of now, it is a worthless piece of paper. Turning it into reality boils down to one thing: *The size of your comfort zone.* No, your comfort zone isn't the villain; its volume is.

A small comfort zone is a plastic cage dropped in the middle of a five-star resort—you're a Peeping Tom in your own life, staring at Michelin-star meals and infinity pools through a glass wall you're too soft to break. In other words, your Backcasting plan remains a fantasy. When your bubble is tiny, you're effectively conscripted into a janitor's closet existence, drooling over a penthouse life that remains strategically out of reach. Staying comfortable is the fastest way to ensure your life remains a microscopic prison of envy.

To claim the spoils of the resort, you must weaponize Momentary Discomfort (The Hard Choice Flywheel) as your primary lever of expansion. Every Hard Choice is a lever that stretches your bubble's frontier. *You aren't aiming to live in permanent pain; you're using temporary heat to forge a larger normal.* Expand the bubble, and the luxuries that once seemed like miracles become your everyday baseline.

Size of your comfort zone equals the size of your life's comfort.

Small comfort zone = Small life. Small comforts.
Large comfort zone = Large life. Large comforts.

Expanding your comfort zone means you expand comfort (Ease) as state of existence.

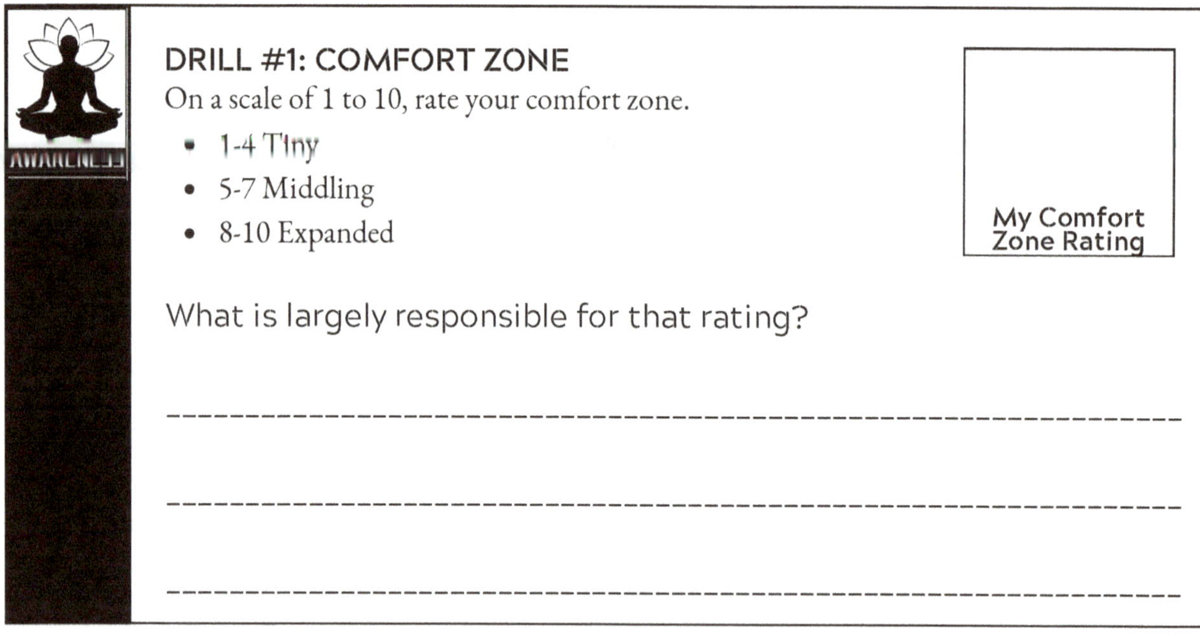

DRILL #1: COMFORT ZONE

On a scale of 1 to 10, rate your comfort zone.

- 1-4 Tiny
- 5-7 Middling
- 8-10 Expanded

My Comfort
Zone Rating

What is largely responsible for that rating?

____

____

____

SMALL SKIRMISHES: EXPAND COMFORT, NEUTER FEAR

If you want to conquer a massive, life-altering fear, you don't start with the boss fight. You start with Small Skirmishes. This is a self-initiated offensive where you proactively pick the fight. The goal is to intentionally engage in minor, highly survivable conflicts that test the outer perimeter of your comfort zone.

Fear thrives on avoidance. What resists, persists. The longer you run from a Hard choice, the bigger the monster grows in your head. Small skirmishes is merely exposure therapy. By stepping into minor discomfort and surviving it, you prove to your nervous system that the danger is an illusion engineered Easy and the ghosts of Pastuality. You aren't trying to conquer the world in an afternoon; you are simply proving to yourself that you won't die from the conflict.

Courage and willpower isn't a genetic gift; it is an exercised muscle built rep by rep.

PICK THE SKIRMISH

Using the list below, pick (3) skirmish items below (1 from each group) to execute an exercise of willpower and as an expansion of comfort zone.

CATEGORY 1: SOCIAL

Goal: Improve communication, lessen social anxieties.

- <u>The Rejection Hunt</u>: Ask for a 10% discount at a coffee shop or retail store for no reason. When they ask why, just say, "Because I'm asking." The goal isn't the savings; it's surviving the "No."
- <u>The Compliment</u>: Find a stranger and compliment something specific and non-obvious (e.g., "That's a great watch," or "Those shoes are bad-ass"). You don't need to linger; deliver and walk away.
- <u>The Story</u>: Next time you're eating at a restaurant with a server, ask the server, "What's your story?" Expand the conversation into their dreams and goals.
- <u>The Convo</u>: Simple... start a conversation with a stranger. It doesn't matter if it ends 10 seconds later.
- Anything else that makes you socially uncomfortable.

CATEGORY 2: PHYSICAL

Goal: Remind your body that it is a servant, not the master.

- <u>The Wim Hof</u>: End your morning shower with two minutes of pure, bone-chilling cold. Stand there and breathe through the torment.
- <u>The One More</u>: At the gym (or a run, or anything with repetition) when your brain screams "I'm done" perform three more reps.
- <u>The Healthy Gag</u>: I drink a foul tasting stew every morning I call my health elixir. Create your own concoction and drink it. Prove you can choose fuel over flavor. I've included my recipe at the bottom of this page.
- Anything else that makes you physically uncomfortable.

CATEGORY 3: THE CAREER STRETCH

Goal: Lean into career/skill discomfort

- <u>The Outreach</u>: Send a DM or email to a hero or high-value lead in your industry. Don't ask for a favor; offer a specific piece of value or a genuine observation.
- <u>The Stage</u>: Be the first to speak in a meeting or the one to bring up a difficult topic everyone else is too comfortable to mention.
- Anything else that makes you uncomfortable.

<u>MJ's Health Elixir Recipe:</u>
- NOT MEDICAL ADVICE. Ask your doctor, this is simply my recipe.
- Low calorie base (Water, fruit juice – 8-10 ounces should not have more than 10g of sugar. I'm not interested in insulin spikes.)
- Added ingredients: Spirulina (3g), chlorella (5g), hemp seeds (2 tbsp), handful of blueberries, turmeric (2g), greens concentration (I use Ancient Nutrition's SuperGreens) tiny dab of bioperine (<.5oo mcg) ... blend and then chug.

MY THREE SKIRMISHES TO ATTACK

Write down each Skirmish you will face, neutering fear, and expanding your comfort zone.

SKIRMISH #1 ____

SKIRMISH #2 ____

SKIRMISH #3 ____

THE PHONE BOOTH PERSONA

In the Shadow War, one underestimated enemy isn't the challenge in front of you, it's the Identity Prison you live in, containing your comfort zone. You've spent years telling yourself you are "shy," "cautious," or 'not the type to lead." That identity is a set of handcuffs that makes Choosing Hard nearly impossible.

The Phone Booth Persona is your strategic workaround. Just as Clark Kent used a phone booth to shed his mild-mannered limitations and reveal the Man of Steel, you will create a specialized avatar designed specifically designed to summon courage and handle the Hard tasks you currently avoid. Think Tyler Durden from Fight Club who went from a mousy pencil-pusher to unapologetic bad ass.

The goal isn't to fake it, but to summon a dormant version of your own potential that doesn't hesitate, play small, and most importantly, doesn't negotiate with Easy and their Brekkian allies. Use often enough and eventually, the mask becomes the face. The Phone Booth Persona and their courage becomes your baseline.

You are who you need to be.

INVENT THE PERSONA

Craft your persona. This is the person who will walk into the room and execute the mission when you feel the fear percolating.

STEP 1: THE CORE TRAITS

What traits does your "Normal Self" lack that this Operative possesses in abundance? (e.g., Ruthless efficiency, unwavering eye contact, zero desire for approval).

TRAIT #1:____

TRAIT #2:____

TRAIT #3:____

STEP 2: ASSIGN A CALL SIGN

A name has power. It must evoke the Hard energy you need.

- Examples: Bulletproof Bob, Iron Sarah, The Closer, Dealmaking DeMarco

Operative Call Sign:_______________________________________

STEP 3: ASSIGN ACTIVATION PROTOCOL

When the Batman skylight flooded the sky, he sprung into action. Your shadow operative needs a trigger that demonstrates you've entered the phone booth. This is a physical or sensory anchor that tells your brain: The standard MJ DeMarco is gone. The bad ass, "Deal-Making DeMarco" has entered the building.

- <u>A Visual Cue</u>: A specific hat, a watch, a leather jacket, a power tie, or a ring.
- <u>An Auditory Cue</u>: A specific song or a whispered phrase (e.g., "Let's roll").
- <u>A Physical Cue</u>: Adjusting your posture, cracking your knuckles, or a deep, 4-second box breath.

Activation Protocol:

____

STEP 4: MISSION DEPLOYMENT

The next tine you need to fire courage and kickstart a Hard Choice, summon your Phone Booth Persona.

- Asking for a raise
- Confronting a difficult situation at work.
- Standing up for yourself.
- Making cold calls.
- Going on stage, public speaking

REWRITING THE PAST

Think of a specific incident where your old self could have used a Phone Booth moment to change your decision, and the outcome.

- <u>The Gag</u>: When you let a colleague talk over you because you feared conflict.
- <u>The "It'll Get Better"</u>: When you tolerated a toxic relationship or a dead-end job for months (or years) longer than your intuition allowed.
- <u>The Frozen Fish</u>: When an asymmetric opportunity appeared, and you watched it sail past because you were "waiting to feel ready."

1. The Incident:

Describe a moment where a Phone Booth Persona would have changed the situation.

____

2. The Cost:

What was the cost of not executing your Persona who gets shit done and takes no BS?

____

3. The Phone Booth Deployment:

If you could send your Phone Booth Persona back in time to that exact moment, what is the one sentence they would have said, or the one move they would have made to flip the script?

____

ACTIVATE PERSONA, ATTACK SKIRMISHES

Activate your persona, and conquer each skirmish you wrote down on the prior page.

SKIRMISH #1: ____

Date Completed _______________________ Victory! (Check)
Notes About the Encounter:

How did it go? How did you feel after? Did you survive?

____

____

____

SKIRMISH #2: ____

Date Completed _______________________ Victory! (Check)
Notes About the Encounter:

How did it go? How did you feel after? Did you survive?

____

____

____

SKIRMISH #3: ____

Date Completed _______________________ Victory! (Check)
Notes About the Encounter:

How did it go? How did you feel after? Did you survive?

____

____

____

Completed all 3? Congratulations—you've just expanded your comfort zone.
Repeat often and soon you'll leave the janitor's closet and expand into resort luxury.

Chapter 14
Time Share Vacation Bliss

You're in Maui, enjoying the sun, when a concierge offers you a free $300 sunset dinner cruise. The catch? You just have to sit through a quick 90-minute presentation. Two hours later, you're trapped in a room being sold a timeshare while suffocating amidst cheap cologne and desperation.

The closer slides a contract across the table for a mild-grade 2-bedroom suite on the beach, but facing the highway. "It's not an expense," he purrs, "it's an investment. And if you sign right now, I can waive the $5,000 activation fee. For only $50,000 and $1,500 for every visit, you'll get two weeks on the tranquil sands of Maui. This offer expires the moment you walk out that door."

Looking at the contract, you think to yourself, "This sounds like a fantastic deal."

REACH INTO THE ARMORY
In order of their effectiveness, ranked 10 for most effective, and 1 for least effective, what decision strategy would help you make the right decision?

Death is in the Details
Examine the contract

Due Diligence
Search for details about the company, timeshare vacations

Genchi Genbutsu
Examine the 2-bedroom suite and its location

Stop, Drop, and Roll
Leave, let emotions subside, and then decide

Stoic Surrender
This opportunity dropped in our laps!

Silva Codebreaking
Meditate, then sleep on it

Rumsfeld Unknowns
Pending lawsuits, timeshare resale markets

Truth Translations
What am I actually buying?

$600 Pizza Test
How much does each visit really cost, especially if we skip years?

Futurecasting
What does it feel like when we don't want to visit Maui for the 13th consecutive year?

DRILL: RUN THE $600 PIZZA TEST

Assume you make the timeshare purchase. For each 14 day visit, it costs $1500. There also are $150/monthly maintenance fees, paid regardless of use. Reality: You estimate to use the property twice every 3 years. After 9 years, you'll used the property 6 times (not even for the full 14 days), or a total of 78 days.

What's your per use cost, per day?　　　　　$_______________

THE MATH

Here is the The $600 Pizza Test with a $50,000 initial outlay, $150/mo, and $1,500 use.

1. The Total Cost (9 Years)
- Initial Outlay: $50,000
- Use Payments Payments: 6 x $1500 = $9,000
- Monthly Maintenance: $150 mo ×12 months x 9 years=$16,200
- Total Cash Out: $50,000 + $9,000 + $16,200 = $75,200

2. The Usage
- Total Trips: 6 (Twice every 3 years, 13 days each)
- Total Days: 78

3. The Real Cost
- Cost Per Trip: $75,200 ÷ 6 = $12,533
- Cost Per Day: $75,200 ÷ 78 = $964/per night

THE VERDICT

With a $50k buy-in, you are effectively paying nearly $1,000 a night to stay in a property you own. This transforms the investment from an expensive slice of pizza into a financial bonfire. You could stay at a 5-star luxury resort for or a posh Pacific Ocean AirBnb at that nightly rate, with zero long-term commitment.

Good decisions are almost never made in the fires of emotion. Scammers, hustlers, and slick marketers know this which is why they weaponize urgency and hype to bypass your logic, hijacking your wallet. If you find yourself in the blast radius of a high-pressure, emotionally charged pitch, your default protocol is to Stop, Drop, and Roll.

Evacuate the room. Let the manufactured urgency to evaporate, and then run the math.

Chapter 15
The Myth of "The Natural"

Several years ago, I fell into a YouTube vortex. I was watching kids in their 20s doing jump rope tricks—crosses, swipes, double-unders. Even though it looked like youthful wizardry, 53 year old me said, "I can do that."

Of course, he bigger question was, ***WHY would I want to?***

The fact was, my VO2 max and cardiovascular fitness was slipping. While I lifted weights with regularity, the intense physical exertion of running or sprinting on a treadmill was absent. The treadmill lets your mind winder into the caves of boredom.

To put it bluntly, I hated the hamster wheel of endurance exercises because they were a neurological lobotomy. In short, they did nothing for my brain. Jump rope did. It requires intense neuromuscular coordination. If your mind wanders, you get whipped in the shins, or worse, the face.

So I bought a rope. I stepped into the gym. And I humiliated myself. I couldn't even jump forward. My brain was wired for roping backward. I was a nearly 60-year-old man tripping over a piece of PVC cord, gasping for air, looking like a coordinated train wreck. My back soon was peppered with red welts from rope-lash. Strangers probably thought my wife was whipping me.

Fast forward to today. Nearly two years later. I am hitting crossovers, running mans, and side-swipes with the speed of a Floyd Mayweather. People at the gym stop and stare at the old man with gray hair and hearing aids and ask, "What's your secret?"

I tell them to read *Choose Hard, Live Easy*, by MJ DeMarco—it changed my life, LOL.

Joking aside, want to know the real secret?

There are (2) of them, and both of them will unleash your power and change your life.

1) THE HARD CHOICE FLYWHEEL

The first secret is the Hard Choice Flywheel, which embodies the process. This is how your Backcasting plan gets real, Chaos is demolished, and your DEFCON/SITREP changes forever.

- Responsibility: My V02 max and cardiovascular endurance is fading.
- Courage: It's OK to look like a stupid old man in public. (I also practiced in private, too!)
- Discipline: To continue practicing when progress slowed to a crawl, or when I "didn't feel like it."
- Discomfort: Fatigue, breathlessness, and of course, whipping my body with the rope.

2) BREAK THE TALENT PRISON

The second secret is the Awareness that you can achieve anything with the right process void of a Talent Prison. The Talent Prison is a cognitive trap in which one believes that Power isn't **earned** but **discovered**. It promotes the fantasy that talent and ability are **events** to be found, not **processes** to be endured. This prison disrespects the most fundamental law of the universe: *Process is Power*. Without the grinding, thankless, power-building process, the glorious event like jump-rope mastery never happens.

- I didn't say, "I'm too old to jump rope."
- I didn't say, "I'm too uncoordinated to jump rope."
- I didn't say, "I wasn't born athletic, why bother?"

I did say, **"With the Hard Choice Flywheel and a dedicated process, I can become whatever I want."**

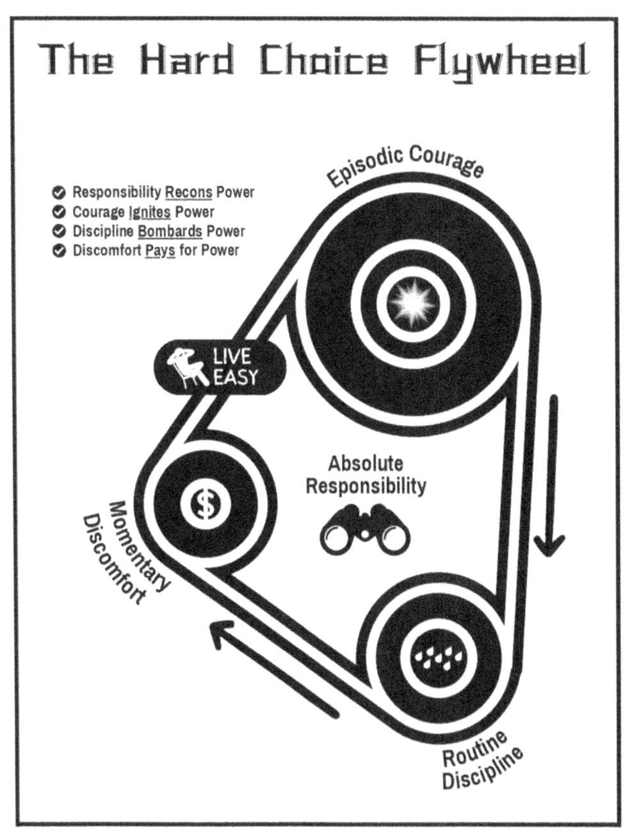

WILL YOUR POTENTIAL GREATNESS DIE IN THE DIGITAL VOID?
Talent is earned, not discovered.
You can become great at anything applying the Hard Choice Flywheel.
The process is courage, discipline, and discomfort.
You can improve your talent by improving your choices.
Chose Hard and stop wishing. Stop waiting. Stop wondering. Start doing.

DEMOSTHENOS DOCTRINE: TALENT IS EARNED, NOT DISCOVERED

In Chapter 8, you committed to (3) Campaign Decisions a signed a contract to reduce your hijacked Awareness, committing to a new skill or talent. Use the Demosthenes Doctrine to turn ONE of these declarations into execution. Complete the (5) Demosthenos Directives to turn your new commitment into a real process backed by the Hard Choice Flywheel

For example, I will play along with my own Campaign Commitment, learning how to play piano.

DIRECTIVE #1: SHIFT EXPECTATIONS FROM EVENT TO PROCESS

Set your Awareness to understand that the Process is the Power. The getting started. The embarrassment and the practice. The reading. The mistakes. What is the process for learning this new talent? Complete the Hard Choice Flywheel.

THE PROCESS: WHAT SHOULD YOU EXPECT?

Responsibility:____

For piano, it's knowing that learning an instrument is great a brain exercise and may prevent dementia.

Courage:____

For piano, it's butchering the keys and finger-pecking Old McDonald Had a Farm.

Discipline: ____

For piano, it's regular practice.

Discomfort:____

For piano, it's regular practice when I don't feel like it because progress feels absent.

THE GROUNDING ANALOGY

Give this process a Grounding Analogy; what familiar process will it feel like?

For piano, I viewed it as a required college course that I must attend to graduate.

The Grounding Analogy: ____

DIRECTIVE #2– DECONSTRUCT THE TARGET.

Demosthenos Principle: Break down the talent or skill into its basic parts.

For piano, that is 20 minutes of practice and/or the simple completion of a song that sounds correct.

THE BASIC PARTS

Break down the skill into its basic parts.

For piano, its chords. Fingering. Reading music.

1) _____________________________   2) _____________________________

3) _____________________________   3) _____________________________

5) _____________________________   6) _____________________________

DIRECTIVE #3– DEPLOY SMGs.

List two small, daily improvements that you can meet that will fire your feedback loop, fuel motivation, and strengthen willpower.

For piano, that is 20 minutes of practice and/or the simple completion of a song that sounds (mostly) correct.

MINIMUM SMALLEST GAINS (SMGs)

What marginal milestones can you set that can fire your feedback loop and motivation?

1) ____________________________ 2) ____________________________

3) ____________________________ 3) ____________________________

5) ____________________________ 6) ____________________________

DIRECTIVE #4– RUN RADAR AND ASSESS PASTUALITY.

After each session, evaluate what worked and what didn't. Refine your approach for the next attempt.

For piano, what's working and isn't? I notice that practice during the day is always more productive than at night.

INTELLIGENCE FROM ACTION

What's working and what isn't?

What's working   What's not working

1)___________________________   1) ____________________________

2) __________________________   2) ____________________________

3) __________________________   3) ____________________________

4) __________________________   5) ____________________________

DIRECTIVE #5– ATTACK YOUR WEAKNESSES

Improve them, don't ignore them.

I enjoy chords and are pretty good at them, but I suck at arpeggios and fingering, particularly using my pinky fingers on distant notes.

WEAKNESSES

1)___________________________   2) ____________________________

3) __________________________   4) ____________________________

5) __________________________   6) ____________________________

FIND AND ENLIST YOUR SCOUTS

Scouts are experts in your field. Books, App tutorials, YouTube channels, etc.

For piano, I purchased several music books and a teaching application.

MY SCOUTS

The following resources will help my journey

1) ________________________________ 2) ________________________________

3) ________________________________ 3) ________________________________

5) ________________________________ 6) ________________________________

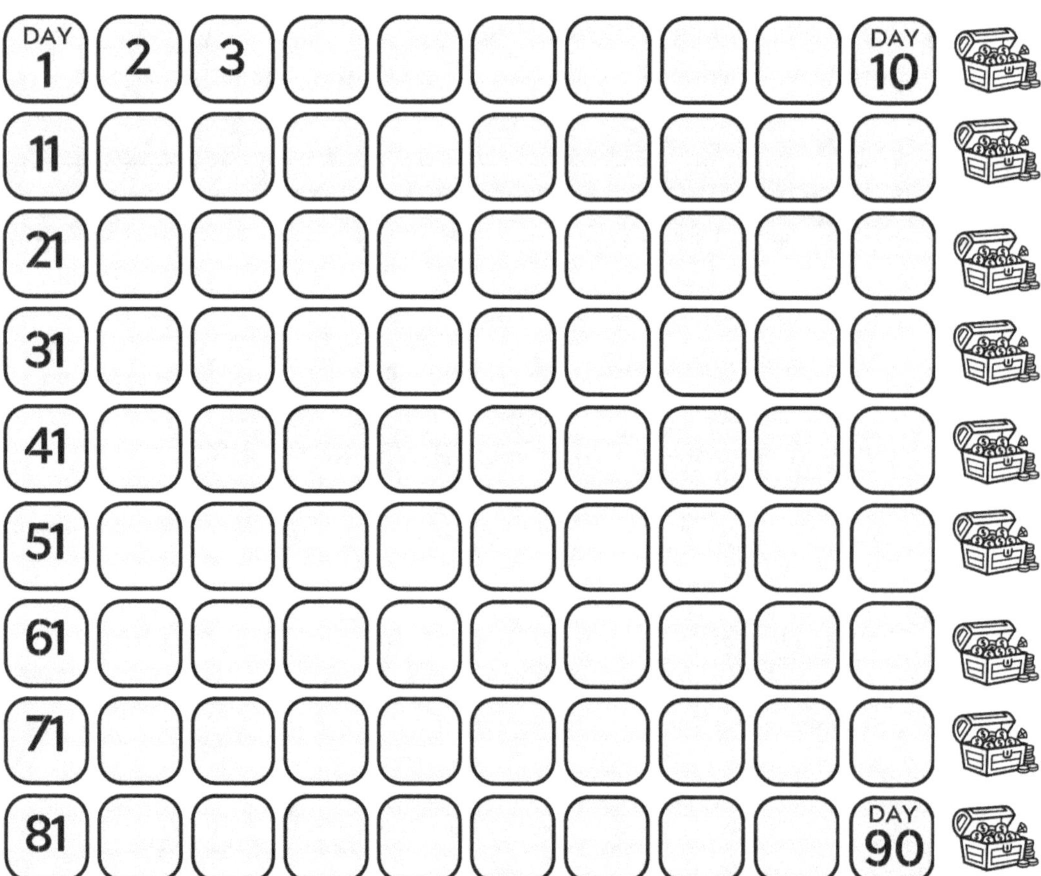

APPLY THE 90-DAY WAR GAME (OFFENSIVE)

Commit to a practicing your skill, hobby, or new talent at least 90 times. Check off each day of completion. After 90 days, you will achieve Power Flow and reach a level of dangerous competence.

MY 90-DAY WAR GAME

Commit to 90 days of process. Check off each completed session, even if the session is only Ten Turns of Momentum. For every 10 days completed, give yourself a reward.

Chapter 16
The High School Reunion

Your 5-year high school reunion is next month. Because you were a high school "nobody," you want to project an aura of success, even though you're broke, jobless, and living with your parents. You're staring down a brand new BMW. You have a great credit score and just secured a 60-month lease at $799/mo—approved only because you committed fraud and lied about your income on the application.*

Note: If these are decisions you'd never make, assume you are convincing your best friend.

FRAME THIS CHOICE THROUGH THE 4 RULES of ENGAGEMENT.

POLARITY: What is the reflective boomerang of this decision? Why?

TRANSIENCE: How long will the high of this choice last?

PERSISTENCE: How long will the consequences/debt last?

IMMINENCE: Am I inviting HARD into my life, instead of delaying it?

FRAME THIS CHOICE THROUGH THE 5 LAWS OF DECISION POWER

MOMENTALITY: Is this the HARD choice?

EVENTUALITY: What are the consequences that might endure?

PASTUALITY: What in my past are influencing this decision?

ASYMMETRY: Am I gambling dollars for dimes? Force multiplier?

INEVITABILITY: Will the decision pave my death with many hardships?

DeMarco's Razor

When faced with (2) Combat Decisions in the fast-pace of life's daily rigors, DeMARCO'S RAZOR is often the best "go to" as it is quick and easy. DeMarco's Razor states that given (2) choices, the HARDER choice is most likely the better choice, given it is responsible.

WEAPONS TRAINING:

Review your decision weapons below. Deploy each weapon to identify and neutralize this poor decision, and an eventual erosion of Power. Use the weapons to help you or your friend get clarity or to give you friend clarity.

First Principle Thinking: Scorched Earth
What is my true, underlying root motive?

____

Stop, Drop, and Roll
What happens if I STOP, let the emotions DROP, and then decide?

____

Worst-Casing WARP Analysis
What is the Worst Case outcome? Asymmetric Risk? Probability influences?

WORST CASE: ____

ASYMMETRY RISK:____

PROBABILITY: ____

Regret Rehearsal + Live in the Skin You've Sewn
Visualize a less than optimal outcome. What does that look and feel like?

DEBT:____

FREEDOM:____

Truth Translations
Give this decision a raw translated truth.

____

Is This Asymmetrical?
What is the force multiplier of this choice? Are you betting dollars to win dimes?

____

The $600 Pizza Test:
What is the per use cost? Are you paying $600 for a $10 pizza?

____

WEAPONS TRAINING, Continued...

Consider a similar financial decision you are making that pre-decides many decisions, like monthly payments. Does it move the needle on your Backcasting plan, or does it move you further away?

Does the Decision Advance My Backcasting Plan? YES NO

Carpe Momentum means to "Seize the Moment" and it is the epicenter of all decision. Forget about Carpe Diem, or Seize the Day. A day is hundreds of moments.

In the Art of War for Decision-Making, a "moment" is defined as 10 seconds because 10 seconds is all it takes to deliberate about a decision, deploy a decision weapon and change your choice.

OUTCOME: THE HIGH SCHOOL REUNION

Turn to the back of the workbook (Dice Appendix) to see potential outcomes for the decision to lease an expensive luxury car.

ANSWERS TO PONDER

- DeMARCO'S RAZOR: The harder choice is to refuse the loan and continue to save money while driving a beater.
- FIRST PRINCIPLES: I'm doing this because my ego is fragile. My friends don't respect me. Why does the opinion of people I haven't seen in 5 years matter more than my solvency?
- STOP, DROP, ROLL: If I get out of the car dealership and wait 72 hours, I'll likely come to my senses.
- WORST-CASE WARP: The repo man. The credit ruin. The shame of losing the car after the reunion.
- REGRET REHEARSAL / SKIN: Fast forward to Payment #42. You are writing a check for $799. The reunion was 3 years ago. You still live with your mom. Feel that check leaving your hand. Feel the crushing weight of the debt every morning when you wake up in your childhood bedroom. The car doesn't even turn heads.
- TRUTH TRANSLATION: I am not buying a car; I am buying a 4,000-pound metal mask to hide my insecurities.
- IS THIS ASYMMETRICAL: I am trading 1,825 days of financial bondage for seconds of perceived validation, either at the reunion or in traffic.
- $600 PIZZA: With insurance, gas, and maintenance, it costs me $32 every hour I drive.
- BACKCASTING: A big financial decision that increases stress and lowers optionality likely does not advance a Backcasting plan.

Chapter 17
The "FOMO" Counterfeit Hard

SORRY, THAT'S NOT HARD, BUT HARD LOOKING FOR EASY

Some Hard Choices are counterfeit. They look or feel hard, but in reality, the alternative is the HARDER choice. Often times, counterfeit Hard choices is the when you are working hard looking for an easy solution, a shortcut, or a foolproof blueprint. Other times, it is knowing when to put the brakes on momentum, even when the momentum is a figment of discipline. (Ex: You come home exhausted and feeling sick—the real hard choice is staying home to get well. The counterfeit hard is going to the gym.)

THE SCENARIO:

For the first time in your life, you are in command over the Shadow War. Your Backcasting plan is ahead of schedule and you minimized Chaos and Hijacked Awareness. You are debt-free. You have a $5,000 Emergency Fund. You have scraped together $20,000 in hard savings. It took you 4 years of saying "No" to vacations, "No" to new clothes, and "No" to expensive dinners to build that nest egg. That money reflects your commitment to discipline.

Now, you want to make it grow. Unfortunately, your Chaos activities brings you to Reddit's WallStreetBets where you see screenshots of guys making $5,000 in a day on a company called Easy Street Enterprises. You look it up. The stock is up 100% in a month. The forum is screaming: "It's going parabolic! To the moon!" Diamond hands are everywhere.

The Fear of Missing Out (FOMO) rages in your head. You feel like the only idiot on earth not getting rich. Desperate to catch the gravy train, you log into your brokerage. You take your $20,000 AND your $5,000 emergency fund—your entire life savings—and hit BUY.

You sit back, heart racing, and give yourself a pat on the back for having such "episodic courage." After reading *Choose Hard, Live Easy*, you guess MJ DeMarco would be proud of your bold move.

THE COUNTERFEIT HARD CHOICE:
"Going all in" feels like a Hard Choice because it's scary. But fear isn't symbolizing a Hard Choice; it screaming recklessness.

- **The Easy Choice**: Betting on "hope" and "free money fantasies" following an anonymous herd because you are too lazy to do the research.
- **The Hard Choice**: Sitting on your hands, missing the hype, and keeping your money safe until you understand the investment.

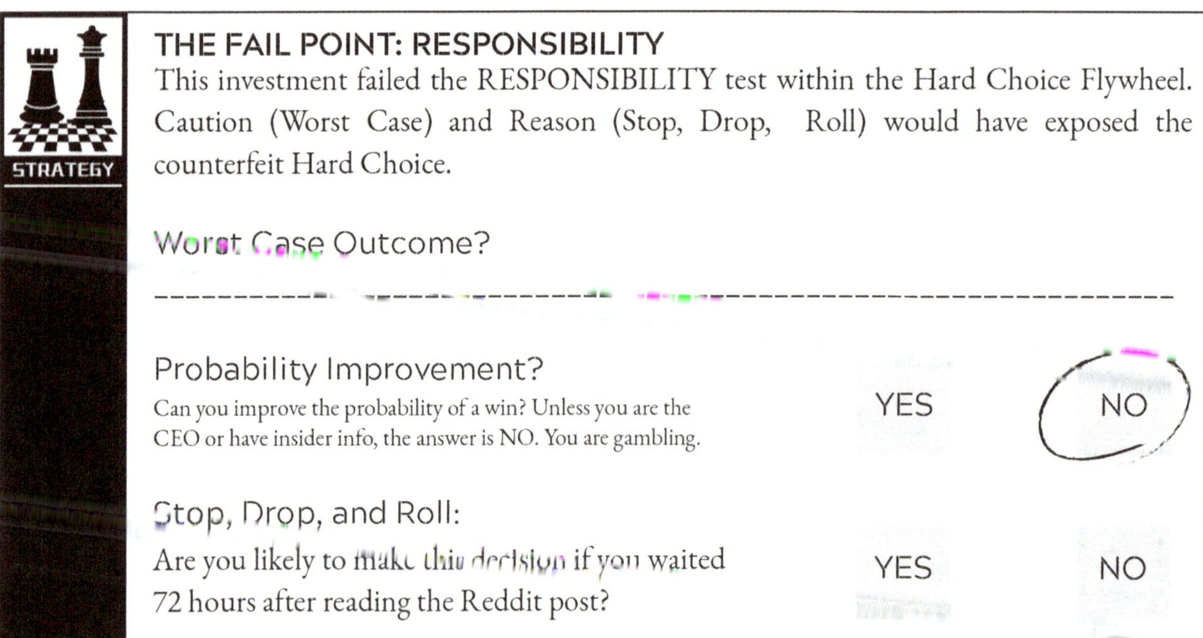

THE FAIL POINT: RESPONSIBILITY

This investment failed the RESPONSIBILITY test within the Hard Choice Flywheel. Caution (Worst Case) and Reason (Stop, Drop, Roll) would have exposed the counterfeit Hard Choice.

Worst Case Outcome?

Probability Improvement?

Can you improve the probability of a win? Unless you are the CEO or have insider info, the answer is NO. You are gambling.

YES   NO

Stop, Drop, and Roll:

Are you likely to make this decision if you waited 72 hours after reading the Reddit post?

YES   NO

WEAPONS TRAINING

Deploy the following weapons to expose this decision as not only a counterfeit Hard Choice, but a bad choice.

THE REGRET REHEARSAL:

Describe the exact moment you realize the money is gone. You are back to $0. It is Day 1 of another 4-year sentence of saving. How does your stomach feel? How do you tell your spouse? How do you tell your kids that Disney will need to wait until they're teens?

THE DUE DILIGENCE DOCTRINE

You relied on Reddit hype. How would you conduct Due Diligence?

Turn to the end of this chapter to reveal the Diligence factors you missed.

GENCHI GENBUTSU (Tour the Battlefield)

How would you conduct Genchi Genbutsu?

Turn to the end of this chapter to reveal the Genchi Genbutsu factors you missed.

HACK THE KITCHEN

How would you "hack the kitchen" to change the calculus of this decision?

Turn to the end of this chapter to reveal the Kitchen factors you allowed.

IS THIS ASYMMETRICAL?

The Counterfeit Hard is the misidentification of the upside asymmetry over the downside. Asymmetry exists on both good and bad outcomes, but they are disproportional. Here's how to sniff it out.

PLEASURE GAIN: (Comfort/Joy) : +100% Gain

What level of pleasure do you gain on a scale of 1 thru10 if you double your money?

$$+1 \quad +2 \quad +3 \quad +4 \quad +5 \quad +6 \quad +7 \quad +8 \quad +9 \quad +10$$

PAIN ENDURED: (Hardship/Regret) : Lose 95%

What level of pain will you suffer when you lose everything?

$$-1 \quad -2 \quad -3 \quad -4 \quad -5 \quad -6 \quad -7 \quad -8 \quad -9 \quad -10$$

The Upside (The Win):

Imagine the stock doubles in one year. You turn $25,000 into $50,000.

- Life Impact: You have a nicer car or a down payment. You feel clever for a week.
- Emotional Voltage: +3 (Cool, but not life-changing.)
- Probability? 1 in 50

The Downside (The Wipeout):

Imagine the stock goes to zero. You turn $25,000 into $0.

- Life Impact: You lose your safety net and 4 years of disciplined saving and their sacrifice. You are vulnerable to any emergency. Job loss. You spiral into depression.
- Emotional Voltage: -10 (Devastating.)
- Probability? 1 in 6

Hint: You are risking a -10 Pain to chase a +3 Pleasure.

This is picking up pennies in front of a freight train, classic gambling dollars for dimes.

THE REALITY
- RUMSFELD: The founder was just released from federal prison for securities fraud. The Reddit posts are from his 6 family members.
- DUE DILIGENCE: You actually read the company's 10-K filing. The company has $0 in revenue. Their business model is a buzzword salad of "Blockchain AI Quantum Manufacturing." It is a vaporware shell company.
- GENCHI GENBUTSU: You drive to the neighboring county to see their "Global Headquarters." The address leads to a rusted, abandoned warehouse behind a strip club. There are no trucks, activity, or employees coming and going.
- HACK THE KITCHEN: Delete Reddit and stop surfing websites that promote Easy, get rich quick fantasies.

VICTIMS OF COUNTERFEIT "HARDS"

Usually when you abdicate Responsibility and embrace a Counterfeit Hard, the are additional victims besides yourself. Below are 5 examples of choices that seem Hard, but aren't responsible. Can you:

1) Name the real Hard Choice?
2) Name the additional victims?

CASE FILE #1: THE "BET ON YOURSELF" BLUFF

You quit your steady job with no savings and no revenue because "Entrepreneurs take risks!" You move back in with your parents to runway your startup.

THE VICTIM: ____

THE REAL HARD CHOICE:____

CASE FILE #2: THE PASSION PIVOT

You're a father who quits his steady job to move his family to Hollywood to pursue acting. He has $0 in savings, no contacts, and no plan. Outside of church skits and an old high school drama class, he has no experience. He says, "I have to show my kids courage, and what it means to chase a dream!"

THE VICTIM:____

THE REAL HARD CHOICE: _______________________________________

CASE FILE #3: THE ALPHA DEFENSE

You're a husband who gets into a fistfight at a bar because a drunk stranger insults your wife. You sucker-punch the guy, knocking him out. He is injured badly and sues your family, but only after you're arrested and spend 6 months in county jail. "I was defending her honor!"

THE VICTIM:____

THE REAL HARD CHOICE: _______________________________________

CASE FILE #4: THE PRIDE HOLDOUT

An unemployed professional refuses to take a lowly job (flipping burgers, Uber, handyman) because "I know my worth." Meanwhile, the family savings hit $0 and he has to ask his elderly parents for a loan to cover his rent.

THE VICTIM: ____

THE REAL HARD CHOICE:______________________________________

CASE FILE #5: THE INSURANCE REBEL

A healthy young man refuses to buy health insurance for his family because "It's a scam and we eat organic." He uses the saved money to buy a nicer car.

THE VICTIM: ____

THE REAL HARD CHOICE:______________________________________

Case #1 - The Victim: Your parents. You are treating their retirement peace as your venture capital. You are outsourcing your living expenses to two people who already raised you. You didn't "buy freedom"; you just changed masters from a boss to your mother. The Real Hard: Keeping the job you hate to pay your own rent, while allocating your 6 -10 PM to build the business until it makes enough money for you to quit with dignity.

Case #2 - The Victim: Your children. You are betting their stability, their school district, and their food security on a lottery ticket. You are prioritizing your ego over their shelter. The Real Hard: Keeping the job to fund the family, while investing your free time to improve your talent (and probability)—only moving once there is a responsible path available.

Case #3 -The Victim: Your wife. She is now left alone to handle the bail money, the lawsuit, and the trauma if her husband gets stabbed or arrested. He prioritized his pride over her safety. The Real Hard: Swallowing your ego, de-escalating the situation, and walking away to ensure she gets home safe.

Case #4 - The Victim: The Parents (again). They are forced to subsidize a grown man's ego. He is protecting his vanity while attacking their financial security. The Real Hard: Taking the embarrassing job to stop the bleeding, while hunting for the dream career at night.

Case #5 - The Victim: The Family, Taxpayers, Hospitals. They are one car accident away from bankruptcy and perpetual insolvency. If tragedy strikes, he will be begging on GoFundMe, effectively asking strangers to pay off his $5,000,000 hospital and rehab bills. The Real Hard: Paying the painful monthly premiums to ensure the family fortress isn't annihilated by a black swan event.

OUTCOME: THE "FOMO" COUNTERFEIT HARD

You fail to do any diligence on the investment and go all in. Your entire life savings. Roll your dice and turn to the back of the workbook (Dice Appendix) to see potential outcomes for your decision future.

Chapter 18
The Curse of Expectosis

Most Campaign Decisions and Backcasting Plans do not die from a lack of ability; they die from Expectosis—a fatal infection caused by unrealistic expectations. When the "Fantasy in your Head" meets the "Brutality of Reality," the collision creates (3) complications:

- The Complication of <u>Unpreparedness</u>: You prepare for sun and find yourself in a thunderstorm.
- The Complication of <u>Resilience</u>: Your mental armor, built for Easy, shatters on impact when Hard appears.
- The Complication of <u>Willpower</u>: With your resilience broken, your energy and will to continue the fight drain to zero.

THE AUTOPSY (PAST FAILURE):
Identify one specific Campaign (Project, Relationship, Fitness Goal) that you quit because it was harder/longer/uglier than you expected.

THE DEAD DECISION CORPSE:

THE SOURCE OF INFECTION:
Who sold you the lie of expectations?

The Highlight Reel: Watching edited YouTube/Instagram videos where the result looked effortless.

The Guru: Buying a course that promised "67 Easy Steps" to riches/abs/love.

The Naivety: Assuming you were special and the rules of friction didn't apply to you.

The Action Fake: I was making myself feel good by doing something trivial, but I never thought about the process I'd needed to commit to.

Other _______________________

THE COMPLICATIONS:
How did the false expectation kill the mission, specifically the (3) complications of misaligned expectations listed below?

(1) UNPREPAREDNESS:
Because I thought it would be easy, I didn't....

____

(2) RESILIENCE:
Because I expected a smooth ride, the first Hard reality caused me...

____

(3) WILLPOWER:
Because meaningful progress was further than what I expected, I...

____

THE 90-DAY WAR-GAME (OFFENSIVE):
Did you execute for 90-days/times before giving up?   YES   NO
(Attempts, practices, sessions, videos)

THE CURE: THE G.A.S.S. PROTOCOL
You cannot proceed without the vaccine. Select one of your Campaign Decisions (Chapter 8) or create a new one. We are going to inoculate it against failure.

THE CAMPAIGN:____

STEP 1: THE GROUNDING ANALOGY (G)
What similar process will this be like? What's already familiar to me?
Frame this journey with a metaphor that implies struggle.

- Expectosis: "Finding a Soulmate is like a Disney movie."
- Reality: "Finding a Soulmate is like digging through a thrift store bin—you have to touch a lot of dirty shirts to find the vintage jacket."

MY ANALOGY:____

STEP 2: THE ATTRITION DOCTRINE (A)

Quantify the pain. Put a number on the rejection. If you expect to kiss 1 frog to find a prince, you are fragile. If you expect to kiss 50, you are bulletproof.

- Expectosis: "I'll post one video and go viral."
- Reality: "I will likely have to post 100 videos to get my first 1,000 subscribers."

MY ATTRITION NUMBER: _______________

STEP 3: THE SCOUT (S)

Find a veteran with scars. Ignore the influencers with BS, filters, and an expensive program to sell. Who has actually done this? What can they tell you about the Desert of Desertion, when feedback is sparse and motivation fragile?

Ex: "Jim found his wife on Tinder, but he told me he had to swipe 1,000 times and go on 20 bad coffee dates first."

POTENTIAL SCOUTS:

(1)_______________________ (2) _____________________________

(3)_______________________(4) _____________________________

STEP 4: SMALLEST MINIMUM GAIN (S)

Fix your dopamine. Stop aiming for the Moon; aim for the 2 inches off the launchpad. If your goal is too big, you will feel like a failure every day until you hit it. Lower the bar to fire the feedback loop and momentum.

- Expectosis Goal: "Find a wife." (Binary: Fail/Success)
- SMG Goal: "Have a 20-minute conversation with a woman where we both laugh once." (Achievable: Builds Momentum)
- Expectosis Goal: "Make $10k/month."
- SMG Goal: "Get one stranger to pay me $1.00."

MY SMG TARGET:____

Chapter 19
Strategic Gratitude

Seminal research indicates that being thankful for the good in your life significantly increases optimism and even lowers physical symptoms of illness. It also has the unusual side effect of enhanced resilience. Low gratitude offenders quit easily, usually when Hard enters the building. In other words, gratitude will help you when the Backcasting plan loses momentum, and "Best You" still seems a distant fantasy.

EXERCISE GRATITUDE, HARDEN RESILIENCE

For only 1 day each of the next 4 weeks, write down 5 things you are grateful for. If you struggle to think of things, simply remove them from your life. What would your life look like? Or, think about things you enjoy today, which 100 years ago where high-class luxuries (indoor plumbing, electricity) were reserved for the world elite. You can only repeat one item per week, so the later weeks require more mental bandwidth!

WEEK #1

(1) I am grateful for: ____

(2) I am grateful for: ____

(3) I am grateful for: ____

(4) I am grateful for: ____

(5) I am grateful for: ____

WEEK #2

(1) I am grateful for: ____

(2) I am grateful for: ____

(3) I am grateful for: ____

(4) I am grateful for: ____

(6) I am grateful for: ____

WEEK #3

(1) I am grateful for: ____

(2) I am grateful for: ____

(3) I am grateful for: ____

(4) I am grateful for: ____

(5) I am grateful for: ____

WEEK #4

(1) I am grateful for: ____

(2) I am grateful for: ____

(3) I am grateful for: ____

(4) I am grateful for: ____

(5) I am grateful for: ____

GRATITUDE GOGGLES

The Gratitude Goggles is a trigger that invokes gratitude. For me, watching tragic stories (like *Dateline*) triggers my gratitude response. Name two actions or behaviors that can help you trigger gratitude on demand. It could be a song, a pet, or movie.

Gratitude Goggles (Trigger #1):

____

Gratitude Goggles (Trigger #2):

____

Chapter 20
The Prisoner's Dilemma?

WEIGHTED AVERAGE DECISION MATRIX (WADM)

Mathematics is the only true universal language. It also is definitive. The number 10 is larger than 2. So when life hands your Backcasting plan a complex fork in the road, try slapping some math onto the decision. The math then becomes a truth serum.

The Weighted Average Decision Matrix (WADM) is a structured thinking tool that converts subjective preferences into objective clarity. It forces you to identify the variables that actually matter, weight them by importance, and score your options against them. This model has been the architect behind every major pivot in my life—from selling three companies to walking away from "can't miss" investments. It strips away the noise and leaves you with a result as undeniable as $10 > 2$.

In the weeds of life's biggest decisions, clarity is godlike. Once the math reveals the superior path, the fear of the Hard choice evaporates, replaced by the confidence to strike. If you aren't willing to do the math, you are choosing to stay blind. Use the WADM to turn the lights on.

For four years, you've been the Alpha-dog at your firm. You have the awards, the $150,000 income, and a mortgage on a house that reflects your status. But the cost is staggering. Your pay is capped because your industry is mature and stagnant. You're also grinding 60-hour weeks. Your weekends don't exist; you recharge on Mondays and Thursdays while the rest of the world is living. You are 25, but you feel 40. Your wife is pregnant, and as the baby's arrival nears, you realize you are a stranger in your own home. You think you're Choosing Hard by continuing the grind.

THE FRONTIER DECISION: You run into a recruiter at a coffee shop who offers you a sales role with XYZ Company in a completely different industry. The starting pay is terrifying—an $80,000 base, a nearly 50% pay cut from your current average. However, the ceiling is $250,000. The recruiter claims the company is solid. Most importantly, the schedule is a standard of sanity: 40 hours a week, Monday through Friday. You get your weekends back. You get your family back. But you lose the certainty of being the Top Dog in an industry you've mastered. Taking the job might endanger your long-term goal of retiring by age 50. You feel it is a choice of two prisons: Prisoner of a job, or prisoner of finances. *What do you do?*

WADM: We're going to grind this decision into a WADM Matrix, but first, I'd like you to recon the decision using several decision weapons.

DECISION RECON

Based on Bayesian Thinking and using current available information, what percentage of confidence do you have that this job offer is a good opportunity, and will improve your life and your family's?

MY CONFIDENCE RATING: | %

RUMSFELD MATRIX:

What are the "Unknown Knowns" in this job offer? Be specific.

Unknown Known #1: ____

Unknown Known #2: ____

Unknown Known #3: ____

	Known to You	Unknown to You
Known to Others	Known Knowns	Unknown Knowns
Unknown to Others	Known Unknowns	Unknown Unknowns

DUE DILIGENCE

List three actions you can conduct to investigate this opportunity to improve decision quality. Be specific.

Diligence Item #1: ____

Diligence Item #2: ____

Diligence Item #3: ____

CANARY QUESTIONS

List 2 Canary Questions and the person to ask that might yield critical decision intel.

Canary Question #1: _______________________________________

Person to Ask: ____

Canary Question #2: _______________________________________

Person to Ask: ____

NEW INFORMATION

After conducting a Rumsfeld analysis, Due Diligence, and Canary Questions, the following new information about the job opportunity surfaces.

1. The recruitment company that offered you the position is well-respected and been in business for 29 years.
2. The company you'd be working sells $3,000 widgets in a growing industry, and has been in business for 14 years.
3. The company currently has 6 salespeople on staff.
4. After posing the Canary Question, "What is the average tenure for sales people currently employed at Company XYZ?" you're told that the answer is 6 years, with 2 of the original 3 sales persons still with the company.

BAYESIAN UPDATE

Based on Bayesian Thinking and using these (4) new bits of information, what percentage of confidence do you have that this job offer is good opportunity, and will improve your life?

My New Confidence Rating: [%]

GENCHI GENBUTSU

Even after your diligence, you're still not sure about taking the new job. You decide to apply Genchi Genbutsu to the decision and visit the company's headquarters.

What would you be looking for? _________________________________

____

____

STOIC SURRENDER

Stoic Surrender is the art of accepting (or taking) whatever life throws at you, and living with flow, serendipity, the "signs of the universe," or "God's plan."

Would you take the new job even
if you hated the idea of it?   YES   NO

If NO, what would need to exist as data or information
for you to say, "YES, I'll go with the flow."

I NEED *THIS* TO GO WITH THE FLOW:_________________________

____

Would you take the new job if you only had   YES   NO
25% confidence it was the right decision?

If NO, what confidence percentage (%)
would you need to take the job offer?   %

FUTURECASTING

Assume you don't take the position. Futurecast this decision 10 years from now, assuming you keep your current job and its hellish hours.

1) Repeated and Compounded:
If I keep my current job and the hours, what does that future look like?

Your mental state: _______________________________________

Your physical state: _____________________________________

Your relationship (spouse): ______________________________

Your relationship (children): _____________________________

Your financial state:_____________________________________

FUTURECASTING (CONT...)

2) Second-Order Consequences:
What other secondary outcomes might spawn from this from this decision to keep my current job?

Your mental state: ____

Your physical state: _______________________________________

Your relationship (spouse): _________________________________

Your relationship (children): _______________________________

Your financial state:_______________________________________

3) Decision Class:
Is keeping this job power, treason, or neutral? Am I gambling dollars for dimes?

Power   Power Flow   Treason   Treason Flow   Neutral

4) Decision Luck:
Is keeping your current stressful job a draw from Luck's Fortune or Death Deck?

Death Deck   Fortune Deck   N/A

5) Truth Translations:
Can you reframe the decision to reflect its likely, future Eventuality? Consider mental, physical and family state. (Ex: Do I want a cigarette = Do I want a seat at the cancer roulette table?)

Truth Translations: _______________________________________

____

____

INTELLIGENCE REPORT:
THE FRONTIER DECISION– NEW JOB OFFER

You have successfully gathered some valuable intel. Much of the decision fog has lifted. The Hard choice now seems less hard. Below is the raw data ready for your thorough WADM Analysis.

- RUMSFELD UNKNOWNS: Average sales tenure and the average compensation. (See below)
- DUE DILIGENCE: The target company has been in business for 14 years and operates in a growing industry.
- DUE DILIGENCE Product: They sell high-ticket widgets ($3,000 price point), implying healthy margins for commissions.
- DUE DILIGENCE: The recruitment firm is highly respected with a 29-year track record, reducing the risk of a bait and switch.
- DUE DILIGENCE: Base Salary: $80,000 (Guaranteed).
- CANARY QUESTION REVEALED: Six sales people currently employed.
- CANARY QUESTION REVEALED: Top performers earn $200,000+.
- CANARY QUESTION REVEALED: The average salesperson earns $121,000 in commission/total compensation.
- CANARY QUESTION REVEALED Retention Signal: Average sales tenure is 6 years. 2 of the original 3 salespeople are still employed (High Stability?)
- GENCHI GENBUTSU: HQ is a Class-A building with high activity.
- GENCHI GENBUTSU: Intercepted a current salesperson in the parking lot.
  - Positive: Driving a Mercedes (validates income potential?). Confirmed "Great place to work."
  - Negative: Mentioned recent layoffs of "bean counters" (administrative staff?). Indicates potential management restructuring.
- DUE DILIGENCE: Key Stakeholder—your pregnant wife is 100% "Go" for this new position.
- FUTURECASTING: Staying in your current role guarantees high stress, zero weekends, and a high probability of "Hellspan" (divorce/strained relationship with child?)
- FUTURECASTING: The new role offers a 40-hour workweek (M-F), returning weekends and evenings to your control.
- TRUTH TRANSLATION: The Cost of Freedom: Assuming I'm average, I am essentially paying $29,000/year (pre-tax) to buy back my weekends, my marriage, and my sanity. Calculation: Current Income ($150k) - New Average Income ($121k) = $29k difference. Net Impact: After taxes, the "fee" for this lifestyle upgrade is approximately $23,000/year.

WADM ANALYSIS

Complete the WADM. Adding your weights and ratings. Some are prefilled based on the current available facts. Do the math and the winner will reveal itself.

- Assign Weights (1-10): How much is "Time with Family" worth vs. "Income"?
- Score Options: Grade your Current Job vs. New Job on each factor.
- Calculate: Multiply Score x Weight for each choice to get the final decision value.

FACTOR	WEIGHT OF IMPORTANCE	KEEP JOB (SCORE)	TAKE NEW JOB (SCORE)
Job satisfaction			
Having weekends back		0	10
Stress / Mental health			
Physical health			
Being a good husband			
Being a good parent			
Commute to job			
Income floor			
Income ceiling			
Rate of pay by hour			
Goal: Retire at 50?			
Ego (Top dog at current co.)		10	0
Job stability			
Industry growth		0	6
Keeping friendships with collegues			
Probability of Hellspan		10	3
Sum Total Scores ---->			

WADM WINNER?

What decision won your WADM Analysis?

I kept the job.   I took the new job.

OUTCOME: THE PRISON CHOICE (JOB OR FINANCIAL?)

Roll your dice, turn to the back of the workbook (Dice Appendix), and select the decision you made to see the potential outcomes for your choice.

DEATH IS IN THE DETAILS

Forget your decision and the outcome you rolled with your dice. Let's assume you Choose Hard, and took the job. You walked away from the golden cage. On Day 1, HR hands you a 15-page employment contract. The font is 8-point and looks standard. You are excited to start, so you commit the cardinal sin of the Shadow War: You sign without reading.

<u>The Reality Check (6 Months Later)</u>
The 40-hour weeks are real, but the potential upside is a mirage. You are grinding, closing deals, and moving units. Yet, your paycheck is stuck at the base salary: $6,600 a month.

You check the contract—the one you didn't read. Page 12, Paragraph 4: "Commission payouts are contingent upon a rolling 6-month probationary period and subject to 'margin threshold' adjustments." Translation: The company can move the goalposts whenever they want. You traded Job Stress (Time) for Financial Stress (Survival). Worse, you think the company is engaged in some type of accounting fraud.

<u>The Parking Lot Betrayal:</u> One afternoon, you see the guy with the Mercedes—the one you interviewed in the parking lot. You ask him how he's crushing his numbers while you're drowning. He laughs. "Oh, my territory is the legacy accounts. My uncle—the owner—set me up with them 14 years ago." Your stomach drops. You do some digging.

- The Top 2 Sales Reps: The owner's nephew (Mercedes Guy) and the owner's brother. Tenure: 14 years each. Income: $250k+.
- The Other 4 Sales Reps: Average tenure: 18 months. Average income: $80k... the base.

The Mathematical Lie: The recruiter didn't lie; he used Weaponized Averages

- (2 Guys @ 14 Years) + (4 Guys @ 1.5 Years) = 34 Years Total.
- 34 Years ÷ 6 Employees = 5.6 Year Average Tenure.

The math was true. The reality was a trap. After 12 months, on pace to make $48,000 less than your old job, you quit.

DEBRIEF: THE AUTOPSY OF A "RIGHT" CHOICE

You used WADM. You chose Hard. You did the due diligence. And you still lost. Why?

LESSON 1: RUMSFELD'S "UNKNOWN KNOWNS"

The enemy (The Company) possessed information that they knew but concealed from you. They knew the "Average" was heavily skewed by nepotism. They knew the contract contained "margin thresholds" that made the $200k ceiling impossible for a new hire.

- The Fix: Never trust an average. Always ask for the median. (The average of 100 people and Elon Musk makes everyone a multimillionaire. The median exposes the truth.)

LESSON 2: DEATH IS IN THE DETAILS (The Contract)

The 8-point font wasn't a printing choice; it was a camouflage tactic. By choosing the Easy path of *signing without reading*, you surrendered your leverage before the first battle.

- The Fix: In the Shadow War, the boring documents are the most dangerous weapons. If you don't read the terms, you don't get to complain about the sentence.

LESSON 3: THE OUTCOME PARADOX

This is the hardest lesson of all. Taking the job was the RIGHT decision based on the available intel. ***You cannot judge a decision by its outcome; you can only judge it by its process.*** You applied logic, diligence, Choose Hard, took a risk for a better life, and acted with courage.

But sometimes, the car still hits you.

Pick yourself up. Update your WADM with new variables (Median vs. Average) and make a new choice. The game goes on.

OUTCOME: THE "NEW JOB" AFTERMATH

Roll your dice and turn to the back of the workbook (Dice Appendix) for the potential outcomes of quitting the new job after new data and experience is revealed.

Chapter 21
The Prison Walls That Jail Us

In the Shadow War for your potential, sometimes your chains aren't fastened by culture or Brekkian drug dealers. You're contained by Cognitive Prisons, a strain of Easy thinking, self-imposed mental boundaries designed to keep you safe, stagnant, and small. If your life feels like it's stuck on a mundane loop, if your Backcasting plan has stagnated, and if your comfort zone remains as small as a shoe-box, you're likely stuck in a cognitive prison.

THE THREE PRISONS

- <u>The Solution Prison</u>: This sector murders your options. You stay trapped with ineffective, Easy answers because the real solution lies behind a wall of discomfort you refuse to climb, or beliefs you refuse to question. *You'd rather fail comfortably than win uncomfortably.*

- <u>The Identity Prison</u>: Here, your identity becomes your DNA, and solutions outside the identity are excused. As such, you sentence yourself to a life that never grows by claiming "that's just who I am." You've traded your evolution for a label, turning your cage into a personality trait.

- <u>The Talent Prison</u>: This wing starves your potential because it attributes talent as innate or natural born gifts. It keeps you a spectator, waiting for a magical spark of talent that never arrives, while the real power—disciplined work—remains quarantined.

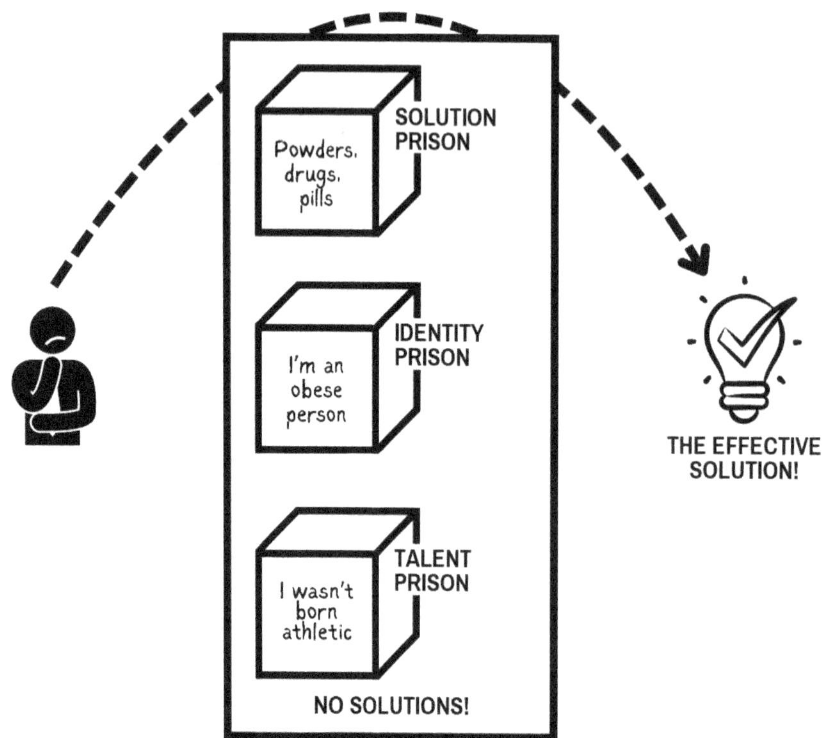

REALITY: The only thing standing between you and your best life is the BS story you keep telling yourself. Prisons serve one purpose: to limit your movement. The escape requires the Hard Choice of taking command and walking through the walls of your own narrative.

THE COGNITIVE CULT

You are 33, but your body feels 63. You are inflamed, overweight, and your joints scream when you climb stairs. You fire the Hard Choice Flywheel and take Absolute Responsibility: "My diet is a dumpster fire of processed trash."

You turn to YouTube. You find a 23-year-old influencer preaching the Carnivore Diet. (Oddly, he claims to be a longevity expert, despite having lived only 15% of a long life). He tells you that vegetables are toxic, cholesterol is a myth, and saturated fat is the nectar of the gods.

THE HONEYMOON: You go all in. You eliminate all processed food, sugar, and seed oils. You eat only chicken breasts, ribeyes and eggs.

- The Result: You lose 20 lbs. Your joints stop hurting. You have energy.
- The Megaphone: You become a zealot. You start an Instagram page. You post videos screaming, "Plants are trying to kill you!" You build a following. You tell your friends they are idiots for eating salad. You are no longer a person who eats meat; you ARE a Carnivore.

THE PLATEAU (Age 38): Five years later, the magic fades. The joint pain returns. The brain fog rolls in. Your libido crashes and you need to take ED medication. You are now insulin resistant; a single grain of rice spikes your glucose to 200. You go to a doctor. He tells you your lipids are terrifying and you are a stroke candidate. A calcium scoring test reveals early arterial hardening.

- The Pivot Point: A rational Bayesian person would say, "Okay, this worked for a while, but now the data has changed. I need to adjust."
- The Prisoner: You do not adjust. You call the doctor a "Big Pharma Simp." You double down.

THE LOST DECADE: For the next 10 years, you chase the old results without changing the diet. You try everything else:

- Cold plunges. Infrared Saunas.
- MCT Oil. Expensive supplements.
- Grounding mats. Hyperbaric Oxygen Therapy.
- Testosterone replacement.
- Pilates, Hot Yoga, Transcendental Meditation

You change 100 variables, *except the one that is killing you.*

SOLUTION PRISON #1: THE FALSE ATTRIBUTION ERROR

Why did you feel great when you first changed your diet? You thought it was because you *added* meat. In reality, it was because you *removed* the poison.

THE MATH OF SUCCESS:

Your Old Life =

[Processed Junk] + [Fast Food] + [Sugar] + [Alcohol] + [Meat] = SICKNESS

Your Diet Change =

[~~Processed Junk~~] + [~~Fast Food~~] + [~~Sugar~~] + [~~Alcohol~~] + [Meat] = HEALTH

THE REALITY:

It wasn't the magic of Porterhouses. It was the *Elimination Diet*. You could have replaced the junk with cardboard and vitamins and likely felt better initially just by removing the inflammation triggers.

THE SOLUTION PRISON:

You fell in love with the Carnivore variable, when the "No Junk" variable was doing 90% of the work. This applies to <u>ANY</u> diet: The juice diet, the vegan diet, the celery diet, the [latest hot] diet.

THE SOLUTION PRISON #2: THE JAIL CELL

With the misattribution of your problem, you've now rigidly defined the constraints of your problem so that the ONLY solution is off the table. You'll never find it because it falls outside the jail cell.

> *"I am willing to do anything to fix my brain fog and*
> *erectile dysfunction... except change my diet."*

Because you have decided that your diet isn't a problem (It made me feel great 5 years ago!) you must look for the solution elsewhere. You spend thousands of dollars and ten years looking for a "phantom variable". Maybe it's mold? Maybe it's 5G? Maybe it's chem-trails? You keep looking in the wrong places, because you refuse to look at the primary variable.

EXERCISE: BREAKING THE SOLUTION PRISON

Think of a problem you have been stuck on for years (weight, health, religious convictions, revenue growth, relationships). What is the ONE VARIABLE you have declared off limits or perfect? (Example: "My business model is perfect, it's the customers who are wrong." "My drinking isn't the problem, it's my stress.")

THE SACRED COW:
What is the variable you've always put "off limits" (diet, religion, city).

____

DO OR DIE:
If you were forced to change this variable for 60 days, or die, could you do it?

YES　　　　　NO

Why?____

UNLIMITED RESOURCES:
If you had unlimited resources (time + money) could you change this variable?

YES　　　　　NO

Why?____

What might happen with Do Or Die or Unlimited Resources?
Does it expose a solution prison, a barrier in your thought process?

____

____

THEN WHAT?
If this variable DOES NOT solve your problem, what have you lost in the process?

____

____

THE IDENTITY PRISON: (BAD)
When "What I Do" becomes "Who I Am."

Why didn't you listen to the doctor who warned you about high levels of LDL and apoB? Because you spent 5 years telling the world you were Carnivore King on Instagram.

- If you change your diet, you aren't just changing a meal plan; you are killing your identity.
- You are terrified of admitting to your 15,000 followers (and your friends) that you were wrong.
- So, you choose to be consistently sick rather than hypocritically healthy.

EXERCISE: THE IDENTITY AUDIT

Where label have you slapped on your existence? (Example: "I'm a Democrat/Republican," "I'm a Vegan," "I'm a Hustler," "I'm a Stoic").

MY IDENTITY LABELS:____

MY IDENTITY LABELS:____

MY IDENTITY LABELS:____

<u>THE GUT CHECK</u>: If new evidence proved that ONE OF THESE labels were hurting you, could you drop it tomorrow? Or would you fight the evidence to protect the label?

For example, I was vegan for 7 years. That's an identity. However, due to exploratory genetic and microbiome testing, I recently was forced (and with great dissonance) to start eating fish a few times per month. So I'm now technically a "pescatarian". What's important is, I didn't let the vegan identity imprison my decision-making or end my Bayesian thought processes. My strategy changed when an Unknown (how do my DNA mutations process fatty acids?) went to Known (not very well).

True sovereignty is having opinions, but not letting the opinions have you.

Bayesian Thinking and the elimination of any cognitive prisons will allow you to make better decisions over time, regardless of identity, beliefs, or talents.

COMMANDER'S VERDICT:

The 38-year-old in this story isn't fictional. It happens every day. We lock ourselves in cells built of "I am…" statements.

- "I am not good at computers."
- "I am a night owl."
- "I am a Carnivore."
- "I am uncoordinated, so I cannot X"
- "I am X, so I can't do Y."

What "I AMS" have you currently locked in a fixed statements of existence?

I AM... ____

I AM... ____

I AM... ____

Burn the "I AMs" and the power-draining identities. Remember the Demosthenos Doctrine. Any talent is within your reach when you embrace the process, embrace the suck, and embrace the truth.

IDENTITY ANCHORS (GOOD!)

Identities could also anchor behavior and steel discipline. Are there any identities that could be helpful to your life, a label that helps you pre-decide behavior and automatically make decisions effortlessly?

- An entrepreneur executes.
- An artist creates art.
- An track and field athlete trains and runs.
- A teetotaler bypasses the cocktails.
- A vegetarian doesn't eat meat.

My Empowering Identity:

____

Chapter 22
The Vampire Retainer

USE S-C-I-R-E TO SOLVE PROBLEMS

SCIRE, Latin for *to know and discern*, is a solution framework that can help solve complex problems. Here is how to use it:

S - Situation... Define the battlefield reality. Stick to facts.

C -Causes... Identify what's creating the problem or preventing victory.

I - Impediments... Map the obstacles, pitfalls, and traps.

R- Rules & Response... Set the Rules of Engagement, the strategy, and the playbook.

E - Execute... Act, Assess, Adjust.

You run a small agency. Your biggest client pays you $5,000/month, accounting for 33% of your total revenue. Per the account manager, they demand weekend Zoom calls, text at 10 PM with emergencies that aren't urgent, and treat your retainer like they own your soul. You're manager is burnt out, resentful, and your other clients are starting to feel the neglect. Worse, they are abusive to your account manager, and the mere sight of their email in your inbox ruins your morning. You know you need to fire them or set hard boundaries, but you keep telling yourself "I can't afford to lose the revenue right now." The money keeps the lights on comfortably, but the stress is causing a tense workplace and some turnover on your team.

What's the Hard Choice? ____

What's the Counterfeit Hard?_____________________________________

Does "Embrace the Suck" Apply Here?   YES   NO

Good decisions are rarely made in the heat of emotion.
Stop, Drop, and Roll is always advised FIRST when emotions are high.
STOP: Pause and allow the emotion to simmer.
DROP: Allow the emotion to drop. 24 hours or more usually suffices.
ROLL: Deliberate post emotional drop.

[S] SITUATION (The Current Reality)

Q: What is the exact situation and challenges facing this conflict?

A:____

A:____

A:____

A:____

[C] CAUSES (The Root of the Infection)

Q: Why did this start? What exactly is creating the friction? Did you fail to set boundaries at the kickoff?

A:____

A:____

A:____

A:____

[I] IMPEDIMENTS (The Prison Walls)

Q: What walls or friction impede a potential solution? Lost revenue? Uncomfortable conversations?

A:____

A:____

A:____

A:____

[R] RULES & RESPONSE (The New Boundaries)

Q: What are the new "Rules of Engagement" that could clear the walls? (Ex: "No texts after 6 PM," "Emergencies qualify as X, Y and Z," "Rate increases by 50% for high-maintenance scope"). Write the specific response you would give if they violate rules.

New Rule: ____

New Rule: ____

New Rule: ____

[E] EXECUTE

You set-up a call with the client and have the Hard conversation, establishing the new rules of the relationship. A good outcome is not assured.

THE $600 PIZZA TEST

You've run the numbers. For $5,000/month, this client takes up 70 hours of service time, plus the second-order consequences of lower staff morale and an employee who quit. The cost to hire and train the new employee was $1,400. Your average client revenue per hour is $475. What does the $600 Pizza Test reveal?

VAMPIRE CLIENT COST PER HOUR: $________________________
(Answers below)

GENCHI GENBUTSU

What's the Genchi Genbutsu move here?

The Move: ____
(Answers below)

OUTCOME: THE VAMPIRE CLIENT

Roll your dice and turn to the back of the workbook (Dice Appendix) for the potential outcomes of this business conflict.

- $600 PIZZA: This client generates $91 in revenue per hour, far less than the average of $475.
- GENCHI GENBUTSU: You are taking your account manager's word. Bayesian confidence that your manager is giving you the situation straight is 75%. To verify, you decide to service the troublesome client for 1 week. You discover the account manager is the problem, not the client.

Chapter 23
The Digital Heist

THE REFUND EXTORTION

A customer buys your digital product, uses it, and then demands a full refund 60 days later (one full month past your strict policy!) The customer seems unhinged and threatens to post negative reviews on social media if you don't comply. The product is only $200, but it violates your principles and the whole idea makes you freaking furious. What do you do and why?

I WOULD:____

WHY ____

Is this a Code of Conduct Violation?   YES   NO

Is This Asymmetrical?   YES   NO

REFUSAL, STICK TO POLICY

If you refuse the refund, would any of the following Rumsfeld Unknowns change your mind?

- The customer is a convicted murderer on parole.
- The customer is a convicted hacker on parole.
- The customer lives 3 miles away from you.
- The customer is a well-known influencer using a burner-account.
- The customer illegally copied your material and is selling it himself.

OUTCOME: "DIGITAL HEIST"

Roll your dice and turn to the back of the workbook (Dice Appendix) for the potential outcomes of this decision.

Chapter 24
The "Family First" Guilt Trip

You have been offered a partnership in a startup that requires moving across the country to a high-cost city. It's a high-risk, high-reward Fastlane opportunity, but it also requires you to invest $25,000, half of your nest-egg. Your family and friends are guilt-tripping you to stay in your dying hometown, saying "family comes first," even though they never seemed to care before. Your current job pays $60,000 a year with a top salary of $100K for top sales performance. Your new job pays the $80,000 but the bigger expenses of the big city make the pay a wash. However, your pay for your partnership is highly variable with unlimited upside. None of your friends are ambitious and their idea of success is a 10 year old F-150 and a trailer down by the river. They're laughing at the lottery ticket you're thinking about buying. You've also been dating someone for two months (appears to be solid marriage candidate) who doesn't want you to leave. What do you do?

What's the Hard Choice?____

Is This Asymmetric?

Upside?____

Downside?____

Run a WORST-Casing WARP Analysis

What's the Worst Case Outcome:__________________________________

Asymmetric Risk Profile:____

Probability Movement: ____

If the "worst case" does happen, "THEN WHAT?"

____

DECISION WEAPONS

Examine each decision weapon and specify HOW they might help you make the correct decision. You don't need to execute the weapon, just answer HOW it helps.

Rumsfeld Matrix: ____

Death is in the Details: _________________________________

Due Diligence: ____

Stoic Surrender: _______________________________________

Expected Value: ____

Canary Questions: ______________________________________

Genchi Genbutsu: ______________________________________

WADM: ____

First Principle Thinking: ________________________________

Pedantic Edgelording: __________________________________

Silva Codebreaking _____________________________________

Regret Rehearsal _______________________________________

Bayesian Thinking ______________________________________

Buridan Buttkick _______________________________________

Eventuality (Skin You Sew) ______________________________

(Turn to the end of this chapter to review how these weapons could help.)

EXPECTED VALUE

Expected Value extrapolates a decision as if it were made millions of times. Calculate the Expected Value of this job offer and move.

Move to New City and Take Partnership	Odds	Outcome
Massive Success	2%	$25,000,000
Great Success	6%	$10,000,000
Modest Success	10%	$500,000
Survival	20%	$100,000
Struggle	22%	$50,000
Total Failure	40%	-$25,000

A positive expected value usually indicates the minimum baseline of a good decision. Higher positives means a better decision, lower negatives, worse. To calculate the Expected Value (EV), of this job offer, multiply each potential outcome by its probability (odds) and then sum the results.

1. Calculate the Weighted Value of Each Outcome:
- Massive Success: 2% (0.02)×$25,000,000=$500,000
- Great Success: 6% (0.06)×$10,000,000=$600,000
- Modest Success: 10% (0.10)×$500,000=$50,000
- Survival: 20% (0.20)×$100,000=$20,000
- Struggle: 22% (0.22)×$50,000=$11,000
- Total Failure: 40% (0.40)×−$25,000=−$10,000

2. Sum the Weighted Values:
$500,000+$600,000+$50,000+$20,000+$11,000−$10,000

Total Expected Value (EV) = $1,171,000

Great Decision: Even though there is a 40% chance of failure and a 22% chance of a undervalued return, the Expected Value is overwhelmingly positive (over $1 million). This is a classic example of upside asymmetry with huge force multipliers, especial since the downside is capped at a $25k loss. The relationship risk, however, is not quantifiable.

OFFER DECLINED: Assume you decline the offer. You learn later that the startup partnership you declined, the owners sold it 3 years later for $1 billion dollars and you lost out on millions. You stayed for "the girl" who ended up leaving you 2 months later. Run the Regret Rehearsal. How different would your life look?

Financial Life:____

Relationship Life: ______________________________________

Lifestyle: ____

OFFER ACCEPTED: Assume you accepted the offer. The proceeds from the business sale nets you $98 million dollars and you never need to work again for the rest of your life. Estimate the Force Multiplier for your decision, assuming you spent 2 years of 50 hour workweeks with only 2 weeks of vacation.

Force Multiplier __________________ TO __________________

Assume you accept the offer and the Worst Case occurs. The business crashes and burns and you're left without a job in an expensive city. What now?

Then What? ____

- Rumsfeld Matrix: What unknowns might make the decision easier? What if you discovered your partner was cheating? Or that the partnership chose you over 9 other partners?
- Death is in the Details: What details might be missing, buried, or inconspicuous? Is there a partner or LLC agreement?
- Due Diligence: What does the company sell? Partner history? Industry growth? AI disruption?
- Stoic Surrender: Does the arrival of this opportunity serendipitously flow with life?
- Expected Value: What is the expected value of this choice if you make the decision 10,000 times?
- Canary Questions: Are there any poignant questions you can use to expose decision details? Customer retention is 90% Or 22%?
- Genchi Genbutsu: Examine the product. Examine the process. Examine the workplace.
- WADM: Examine the two decisions in accordance to your priorities and values.
- First Principle Thinking: What is your root motives for taking or declining the job? Are you really looking for an exit from your relationship? An exit from family drama? Get rich?
- Pedantic Edgelording: What is the cringiest thing about this proposition?
- Silva Codebreaking: Think on it, then sleep on it and see what your subconsciosu says.
- Regret Rehearsal: Feel the regret of all the outcomes: Company sold for billions, losing a potential life partner.
- Bayesian Thinking: What confidence do you have this is a great opportunity?
- Buridan Buttkick: Does this break momentum of the status quo?
- Eventuality (Skin You Sew): What do the various futures look like, and how do they feel? Are you risking a 4 life for a 10 life?

OUTCOME: "FAMILY FIRST"
Roll your dice and turn to the back of the workbook (Dice Appendix) for the potential outcomes of this decision.

Chapter 25
The Subscription to 'Sucks' You Didn't Want

THE PERSISTENT ENTREPRENEUR

You have spent 18 months and $15,000 trying to launch a subscription box service. To date, you have 19 subscribers and are profiting $40 a month while working 30 hours a week. You tell yourself that "persistence is key" and that you just need one big break. Tons of people say they "love the idea" but sales never seem to come.

DECISION WEAPONS

Embrace the Suck ... Does It Apply?	YES	NO

Why or Why Not? _______________________________

The $600 Pizza Test... Does it Apply?	YES	NO

Why or Why Not? _______________________________

Zero-Based Thinking... Does it Apply?	YES	NO

Why or Why Not? _______________________________

Act, Assess Adjust... Does it Apply?	YES	NO

Why or Why Not? _______________________________

Monkey First... Does it Apply?	YES	NO

Why or Why Not? _______________________________

What's the Hard Choice?_______________________________

What's the Counterfeit Hard? _______________________________

ANSWERS:

Embrace the Suck: No: It seems to apply, but it doesn't as the other decision weapons will prove.

$600 Pizza Test: Yes: Even though this isn't a purchase decision, it is a per unit calculation. You are working for less than minimum wage, and look to continue to do so.

Zero-Based Thinking: Knowing what you know now, you'd never start this business... so why continue?

Act, Assess, Adjust: Yes, but the entrepreneur doesn't look to have used it. After a few months, this project should have been abandoned when continual adjustment yielded no sales or responsiveness to messaging.

Monkey First: Yes, clearly there is a bottleneck, or a problem with the product or the messaging. After 18 months, it hasn't been solved. Pedestal built, juggling monkey still dropping flaming torches.

Chapter 26
The "I Deserve It" Trap

You just received a promotion that bumps your salary by $15,000. Your current car is 10 years old, paid off, and runs fine, but it's an eyesore. You've been eyeing a Mercedes luxury lease that costs $999/for 48 months. It fits within your new budget, and you feel you deserve it for your hard work and being debt free. You're 33 years old with no retirement savings, engaged to be married, and on the fast-track for executive management. You told yourself that the hot ride will increase your sales performance. Your short term goal is home ownership, followed by a long-term goal of retirement by 55. You're about to pull the trigger... does any decision weapon change your mind?

Is This Decision Asymmetric?   YES   NO   MAYBE

Why or Why Not? ____

What does **First Principles** Say About Your Motives?

(1)____

(2)____

Futurecast This Decision
A) Repeat and Compounded
This is one decision the creates 48 other decisions. What does that look and feel like?

____

____

B) Second-Order Consequences:
What other consequences might appear downstream? Cover both good and bad.

(1)____

(2)____

(3)____

C) Slow the Moment: Classify the Decision

Power   Power Flow   Treason   Treason Flow   Neutral

Truth Translation:
Give the decision a Truth Translation to expose its bare reality.

____

Pedantic Edgelording
What would an internet troll or a Red-Team Audit say about this decision?

____

WWJD: What would your hero or favorite mentor advise?

____

OTHER DECISION WEAPONS
Every decision weapon below could help you make the right decision, except ONE.
Identify the relevant ones (including WHY) while exposing the tool that isn't relevant.

WADM (Why it might help): ____

The Atomic Domino (Why it might help):_____________________________

$600 Pizza (Why it might help):____________________________________

Genchi Genbutsu (Why it might help):_______________________________

Hansei (Why it might help): _______________________________________

OUTCOME: THE PROMOTION GIFT
Roll your dice, remember your number, and turn to the back of the
workbook (Dice Appendix) for the potential outcomes of this decision.
Also, get the answers for some of the questions posed above.

The Atomic Domino strategy is the irrelevant framework. WADM will triage the decision, $600 Pizza will give you
per use cost, Genchi Genbutsu will help you discover owner issues or problems, and Hansei might expose what
bullshit in your past is making you consider this purchase.

Chapter 27
Juggling Zeroes And Lit Dynamite

Congratulations. You created a Backcasting plan in this workbook 7 years ago and it all came true. You worked your ass off. Expanded your comfort zone. Eliminated Chaos. Hacked Kitchens. Cured Expectosis and abolished the cognitive prisons. You become a walking embodiment of the Hard Choice Flywheel. And then with one decision—one moment— you completely destroyed your life. A Zero drops.

There are some decisions where the downside is not just painful—it is a complete annihilation. I call this Nuclear Treason or a DAREs; Downside Asymmetrical Risk Events where you are are gambling with infinite (or permanent) downside (death, prison, paralysis, ruin) for capped, limited upside (A buzz, a laugh, a few "likes"). This concept is called Juggling Zeroes because this one Easy decision is like multiplication by zero. Great decisions add. Your Backcasting plan is all addition. Nuclear treason multiples by ZERO and erases all good decisions.

<u>Example</u>: You're a pro baseball player making millions. But you decide to drag race your Ferrari on a city street and you crash, killing a family of four. Zero. 30,000 hours of training is erased. Prison. Life ruined.

THE DRILL:
Evaluate the scenarios below using these two scoring parameters: 1) Chance of Ruin and Hellspan.

CHANCE OF RUIN (1–10):
How probable is the catastrophic outcome?

- 1 = Rare, but not impossible. (1 in 10000)
- 2 = Unlikely (1 in 1000)
- 5 = Moderate Risk (1 in 250)
- 7 = High Risk (1 in 100)
- 9 = Severe Risk (1 in 50)
- 10 = Catastrophic Risk (1 in 25)

HELLSPAN (1–10):
If it goes wrong, how long does the suffering last?

- 1 = A bad weekend.
- 2 = A bad week
- 5 = A bad month
- 7 = A bad year
- 9 = A bad decade
- 10 = A coffin, a wheelchair, or a prison cell.

If you perform an action with a 4% risk of ruin just 18 times, you have a greater than 50% chance of total catastrophe ($1-0.96^{18} \approx 52\%$).

In the context of a lifetime of decisions, a 1-in-25 risk isn't just high—it is a mathematical certainty of destruction. This is why I continue to curse motorcycling on public roadways with distracted drivers. One ride likely won't kill you. One hundred rides will. Bad decisions compounds and Hellspan awaits.

THE BODY SHAME: You film an old woman changing in a gym locker room, mock her body, and post it on social media

THE PASSENGER: Your boyfriend buys a motorcycle. He is a high-adrenaline show-off. He says, "Hop on, babe."

THE BUZZ: You've had 5 beers at happy hour. You feel *fine* to drive the 13 miles home.

THE DOZE: You are 12 hours into a road trip. Your eyes are heavy, but you push to make the next town.

THE VENT: You hate the President. You post a *joke* about assassination on social media.

THE PROTEST: You are angry at a policy. You drive your car into a crowd/officer to "make a statement."

THE JARED: You scream at a teenager working at drive-thru because of their company's politics and post the video online.

THE DRAG RACER: You race a Honda Civic in your 650 HP Viper after 3 cocktails.

THE SPEED RUN (LITE): You hit 120 mph in your Lambo on a deserted highway at 2 AM.

THE SPEED RUN (HEAVY): You hit 120 mph in your Lambo, weaving through traffic at 2 PM.

THE AFFAIR: You have a loving spouse and 3 kids. You sleep with your boss during a conference.

THE STUNT: Seeking viral fame, you video yourself jet-skiing on a folding table pulled by a truck.

THE TOURIST: You pay $250k to dive to the Titanic in an experimental, uncertified carbon-fiber submersible.

THE SAMARITAN: An intoxicated vagrant on the street is vandalizing cars and you try to stop him.

THE HERO: An man looks to be kidnapping a child on the street, you decide to intervene.

THE KNIGHT: A man is beating his wife outside a restaurant. You intervene.

THE DEFENDER: A woman is flirting with your husband. You decide to cold-clock her across the face with your martini.

THE ENTREPRENEUR: You decide to sell counterfeit goods imported from China because of irresistible margins.

THE EMPATHIC DRUG DEALER: Not legal in your state, you decide to sell MDMA to PTSD patients as treatment.

THE PARTNER: You start a business with a guy who just got out of prison for fraud/murder "on a technicality."

THE DARE: At a garden party, friends dare you to eat a live slug crawling on the patio.

THE INSIDE MAN: Your pro-athlete buddy gives you "inside info" on a game. You bet the house.

THE ACCOMPLICE: Your friend offers you a cool 20% to be the driver for a quick convenience store robbery.

THE TOUGH GUY: You have unusual abdominal pain. Cancer is in your family DNA. You "tough it out" and skip the doctor.

THE COMMUTER: You buy a motorcycle to commute 16 miles on the freeway in rush hour, 5 days a week.

THE VIGILANTE: Someone insulted you online. You drive to their house with a loaded AR-15 to "talk."

THE HARD REALITY OF "ZERO" KILLING ASYMMETRY

Did you read some of these and laugh? Did you roll your eyes at a 2% chance (Chance of Ruin: 1 in 50, 9, Severe Risk) at catastrophe? Again, if a bowl of 1000 jelly beans contained 2 arsenic-laced killers, would you reach into the bowl and eat? Wake up. Many of the scenarios above are not hypotheticals, but true stories of people who Juggled Zeroes and dropped them.

- The Slug: In 2010, 19-year old Sam Ballard ate a garden slug on a dare. He contracted rat lungworm disease, fell into a coma for 420 days, and woke up paralyzed with severe brain damage. He required 24/7 care until he died 8 years later. Hellspan: 10.
- The Submersible: The Titan Submersible imploded instantly, killing all 5 passengers who paid a fortune. The owner bypassed safety regulations and fired whistleblowers. Hellspan: 10.
- The Body Shamer: A Playboy Playmate posted a photo of a naked elderly woman at the gym. She was charged with a crime, lost her job, career, and became a global pariah. Hellspan: 9.
- The Viper: This was me. I drove my Viper drunk. I crashed and nearly killed myself, drawing from the Death Deck and juggling Zeroes. If I had killed someone, I would be writing this from a cell block—or not writing it at all.

EXPOSE THE ZERO:

Examine your life. Where are you juggling zeroes? What feels like a low probability (2%) but if you did it 50 times, it suddenly becomes a predictable outcome? It doesn't matter if the probability is low. If the Hellspan is "Life in Prison" or "Quadriplegic," these are bets that should be avoided. Betting $10,000 to win 2 cents is a bet for morons. Stop juggling zeroes. Eventually, gravity wins.

#1 Potential 0 Behavior: ____

#2 Potential 0 Behavior: ____

#3 Potential 0 Behavior: ____

END THE ZERO

Pick one ZERO you've identified and make a HARD Choice to end the behavior.

The Hard Choice: ____

OUTCOME: MESSING WITH THE DEATH DECK

Pick one behavior above that you identified as Juggling a Zero. Roll your dice TEN TIMES. If you get a "snake eyes" just once, you dropped the ZERO and Hellspan awaits. Avoid the snake, and dumb luck prevails.

Chapter 28
The Walking Dead: Origin Story

DIRECTIONAL PROBABILITY

Everything is connected. Your past, your memories, your decisions, their aftermath. The lies you feed, and the truth your ignore. When the train left the station, derailment was nearly impossible, a low probability. Then slowly, one by one, the chances of a devastating crash goes up, one by one, and slowly day by day through poor decision making. And finally, a 1000 miles away from its embarkment, or in our case, 5 or 10 years later, the trainwreck is complete. Here's how Directional Probability works. Every time you drive a car, there is risk of death or accident, many times no fault of your own.

Action	Chance of Driving Disaster	Luck (High-Fortune) (Low-Death)	Probability Boost
Decide to visit a friend 30 miles away. You hop into your car.	.0005%	High / Fortune	N/A
Fasten seat belt.	.0001%	High / Fortune	Boosted for Good Outcome
Sitting in your car before leaving, you decide to smoke a little weed.	1%	Low / Death	Boosted for Bad Outcome
You also slam three beers before starting the engine.	4%	Low / Death	Boosted for Bad Outcome
Speed over limits by 30 mph.	11%	Low / Death	Boosted for Bad Outcome
The police have fired their lights and want you to pull over. You ignore them and gun it.	40%	Low /Death	Boosted for Bad Outcome
You run every red light/stop sign.	80%	Low / Death	Boosted for Bad Outcome

Your decisions matter. While you can't see the odds, or the probabilities, they indeed boost the odds of certain outcomes. Winners understand these battlefield physics. Losers ignore them and instead choose to punch themselves in the face, often left to wonder, "Why is my faced so bruised?"

THE SCENARIO: THE WALKING DEAD

Here's why directional probability matters in all things. Let's say you were laid off from a big corporation and given no good reason. You were a good worker and thought yourself as valuable. But suddenly, the chances of becoming a "loser" start to move...

Action / Inaction / Thought	Chance of Being a Loser	Luck (High/Low) (Fortune/ Death)	Probability Boost
I was laid off, WTF? I was a great worker!	.0005%	High / Fortune	N/A
STAGE 1 — Rumsfeld Unknowns / Death in the Details: Choice...You don't investigate your dismissal, which would have revealed that you were indeed a top 10% employee. You were laid off due to a pending, unannounced merger.	.0001%	Low / Death	Boosted for Bad Outcome
STAGE 2 — Sabotage Pastuality: Belief... "I must not be a good worker. I'm not valuable. Corporations suck."	1%	Low / Death	Boosted for Bad Outcome
STAGE 3 — Dirty Kitchen / Theater of Chaos: Choice...You seek communal comfort in the digital basements of r/antiwork or similar subReddits. Victim rants are applauded and upvoted. You aren't seeking solutions; you're seeking a defeated tribe to validate your misery.	9%	Low / Death	Boosted for Bad Outcome
STAGE 4 — Identity Prison / Hijacked Awareness: Choice... You spend 4 hours a day marinating in "the system is rigged" rhetoric. Your awareness is hijacked; your identity is no longer "valuable" but "victim." You have locked yourself in an Identity Prison where the bars are made of upvotes from people who have already surrendered.	17%	Low / Death	Boosted for Bad Outcome
STAGE 5 — The Solution Prison: Choice...You land a new job, but you've smuggled your new identity and memory of your last failure into the new building. You decide to "Quiet Quit" before you even start. "Why bother? The game is rigged, right?"	24%	Low /Death	Boosted for Bad Outcome
STAGE 6 — Expectosis: Choice...Your resilience vanishes as you expect the world to be a meaningless, rigged wasteland. The first time a boss gives you feedback or a project gets difficult, you crumble. Your willpower is bankrupt because you've convinced yourself that effort is futile. 24 months ago you had self-worth. Today, you're 33 years old and living in mom's basement.	40%	Low /Death	Boosted for Bad Outcome

DECISIONS, MEMORIES, AND KITCHENS MATTER.

The path to becoming another one of life's walking dead isn't an overnight phenomena. It happens one decision, one memory, one visit at a time. Each of these decisions felt Easy, even rewarding, in the moment. It's easy to complain on X or BlueSky. It's easy to blame "the system." It's easy to do the bare minimum at work. But these choices are high-interest loans that stack bad probabilities, handing you life's Death Deck of Luck.

By the time you reach Stage 6, you haven't been unlucky. You have spent months engineering your own self-inflicted trainwreck. You didn't just end up broke and unemployed in a basement; you conscripted yourself into that life through a series of directional maneuvers that made any other outcomes unlikely.

What decisions are you currently making that are boosting the hidden probabilities of bad outcomes and a tattered skin you must wear?

DECISIONS (Momentality)

What decision or beliefs are currently moving <u>Directional Probability</u> in the wrong direction, sabotaging your chances for a better life?

(1) ________________________________(2) ________________________________

(3) ________________________________ (4) ________________________________

MEMORIES (Pastuality):

What memories are moving probability, sabotaging your chances for a better life?

(1) ________________________________(2) ________________________________

(3) ________________________________ (4) ________________________________

ENVIRONMENTS (Kitchens):

What dirty kitchens are you hanging out in? Social media apps? Subreddits? Facebook groups? Loser friends? Fast food joints rife with grease and inflammation?

(1) ________________________________(2) ________________________________

(3) ________________________________ (4) ________________________________

KITCHEN HACKS

Circle 1 item each, from Decisions, Memories, and Environments that you will seek to resolve using Act, Assess, Adjust.

Chapter 29
Operation Red Pill

The enemy combatants of the Shadow War are hidden in plain sight. But most people refuse to open their eyes to the reality that faces them. You think you're just driving to work? Listening to the radio or watching a basketball game? Wrong. You are witnessing a multi-billion dollar bombardment designed to recruit you into the Cult of Easy.

THE TARGET LIST (THE 5 ARCHITECTS)

Before you deploy, memorize the faces of the enemy. They do not want you healthy, wealthy, or wise. They want you sick, broke, angry, divided, and distracted.

 <u>Big Food</u>: The Architect of Obesity & Disease
Weapon: Comfort, Addiction

 <u>Big Finance</u>: The Architect of Debt
Weapon: "Low Monthly Payments"

 <u>Big Pharma</u>: The Architect of Dependency
Weapon: The Quick Fix Pill, Dependence

 <u>Big Media</u>: The Architect of Distraction
Weapon: Outrage, Dopamine, Circuses

 <u>Big Education</u>: The Architect of Obedience
Weapon: Mediocrity, Victimhood, Good Employee

THE MISSION: 24-HOUR RECON

Act as a spy for Team Hard. Your objective is to identify the Easy traitors hiding in plain sight. These are enemies actively encouraging Easy, poor choices that work with the Cultural Cartel. For the next 24 hours, your mission is to identify the Easy traitors hiding in plain sight. Every time you see an attempt to seduce you into the trap of Easy; laziness, distraction, gluttony, debt, or stupidity, log it on the next page.

- **Your Drive to Work:** Count the fast-food signs. Count the billboards: plastic surgery, injuries lawyers promising huge payouts for fender benders.
- **The Radio:** Listen to the ads for debt consolidation, miracle drugs, fast food, or processed junk.
- **The Office:** Spot the sugary snacks (vending machines, breakrooms) used to pacify the workforce.
- **The Screen:** Note how many times your phone tries to steal your attention.
- **The Television:** Note how many commercials are pushing trash, from alcohol, to fast food, to some new reality TV show designed to manipulate your Awareness.

LOGGING PROTOCOL:

- <u>The Agent</u>: Who is attacking? (e.g., McDonald's, Credit Card Co., News Channel)
- <u>The Weapon</u>: What is the specific message? (Ex: "You deserve a break today," "0% APR," "Breaking News Panic")
- <u>The Trap</u>: What is the actual Easy choice they want you to make? (Ex: "Eat poison," "Spend money I don't have," "Get angry at strangers")

SURVEILLANCE LOG:

Time	Source	The Product and Message	Cartel
830 AM	Radio	Drug | Fix your diabetes!	Big Pharma

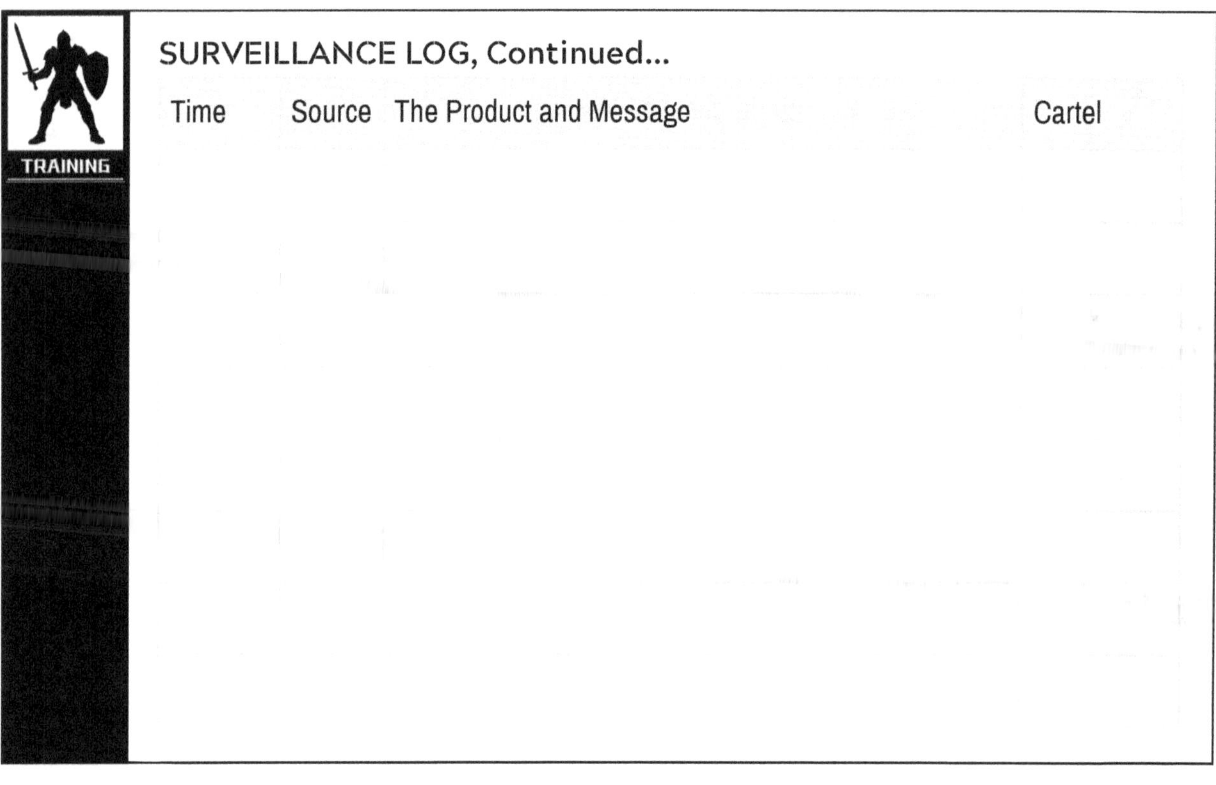

SURVEILLANCE LOG, Continued...

Time	Source	The Product and Message	Cartel

THE AFTER-ACTION REPORT
Once the 24-hour surveillance is complete, review your intel.

The Bombardment Count:
How many total attacks did you log in a single day?   Count:

The Matrix Moment:
Now that you see it, you can't unsee it. Does this change
your perspective on the gravity of the war?   YES   NO

CONCLUSION
The last chapter in this workbook is purposeful. It is a reminder that your Culture isn't your confidant; it's a predatory pimp peddling the poison of Easy to keep you pacified, predictable, and profitable for the machine. Every day is a relentless barrage of solicitations designed to dissolve your discipline and disarm your intent. Make no mistake: this is a Shadow War, and the lawless Wild West of the modern world has no mercy for the defenseless. If you aren't actively Choosing Hard, you aren't chilling—you're being processed and monetized. Strap on your armor, sharpen your discernment, and remember that in the Art of War for your life, the only way to win the spoils is to refuse the seduction of the soft.

The Oath of the Unconquered

I hereby renounce the seductive siren of Easy and the poisonous assault of a culture designed to keep me compliant, comfortable, and ultimately, inconsequential. I recognize that every morning is a tactical deployment into a world that wants my discipline dissolved and my sovereignty surrendered. From this moment forward, I am the Supreme Commander of my choices and the sole architect of my outcomes. When the moment strikes and the path splits, I will not flinch, I will not forage for excuses, and I will not trade my future greatness for a fleeting, mediocre Now. I choose the Hard today so I can own the Easy tomorrow. I acknowledge that war is relentless and constant, the stakes are my life, and I intend to win the spoils... affluence, legacy, love, health and happiness.

SIGNED:____

DATED:____

Appendix A
Your Decision Armory

- $600 Pizza Test – 293
- 1/2/3 Divorce Defense – 257
- 3As – 309
- 90 Day War Game (Def) – 137
- 90 Day War Game (Off) – 137
- Ad Blitz Razor – 277
- Atomic Domino – 314
- Attrition Doctrine – 166
- Backcasting – 217
- Bayesian Thinking – 306
- Big Ugly Funeral – 10, 63
- Buridan Butt Kick – 282
- Business in a Box Razor – 277
- Canary Questions – 250
- Death is in the Details – 243
- DeMarco's Razor – 277
- Demosthenes – 175
- Directional Probability – 183
- Do or Die – 170
- Due Diligence – 239
- Edgelording – 269
- Embrace the Suck – 151
- Eventuality: Live in Its Skin – 64
- Expected Value – 295
- FICK – 143
- First Principles – 254
- Force Multiplier – 79
- Funk Buster – 271
- Futurecasting – 290
- Genchi Genbutsu – 252
- Gratitude Goggles – 149
- Grounding Analogy – 166
- Hack the Kitchen – 142
- Hansei – 267
- Headline Razor - 278
- I am Who I Need to Be – 172
- Identity Anchors – 138
- Is This Asymmetrical? – 300
- Juggling a Zero (DARE) – 78
- Kaizen Chess – 223
- Life As – 215, 229
- Luck's Fortune / Death Decks – 177
- Maestro Visualization – 150
- Memory Alley – 140
- Metaphorical Lensing – 280
- Momentality Detox – 317
- Monkey First – 312
- North Star Offensive – 102
- Pain is Intel – 150
- Phone Booth Persona – 129
- Pivot and Point – 132
- Poison Candy Gambit – 185
- RADAR – 61
- Regret Rehearsal – 130
- Revenue Razor –
- Rumsfeld Matrix – 247
- SCIRE – 274
- Sellout Razor – 277
- Silva Codebreaking – 288
- Slow the Moment – 50
- Small Skirmishes – 132
- Smallest Min Gain (SMG) – 141
- Standing Orders – 139
- Stoic Surrender – 285
- Stop, Drop, and Roll – 122
- Talk Some Sense to Him – 68
- Talk to the Shadow – 136
- Ten Turns – 143
- The Gun + $10M Question – 104
- Theaters of War, Power + Intel – 107
- Then What? – 131
- Thinking Razors – 277
- Tombstone Razor – 278
- Trigger Strategy – 144
- Truth Translations – 260
- WADM – 302
- Willpower Bootcamp – 99
- Worst Case WARP Analysis – 121
- WWJD – 129
- YODO – 74
- Zero-Based Thinking – 171

Appendix B
Behavioral Index of Decision Weapons

A
Addictions, Overcoming
- Big Ugly Funeral 10
- Slow the Moment 50
- Eventuality: Live in Its Skin 64
- Talk Some Sense to Him 68
- Force Multiplier 79
- Willpower Bootcamp 99
- The Gun+ $10M Question 104
- Theaters of War, Power 107
- WWJD 129
- Regret Rehearsal 130
- 90 Day War Game (Def) 137
- Identity Anchors 138
- Standing Orders 139
- Hack the Kitchen 142
- Ten Turns 143
- Do or Die 170
- "I am who I need to be." 172

Ambiguity, Gaining Clarity
- Worst Case WARP Analysis 121
- Due Diligence 239
- Death is in Details 243
- Rumsfeld Matrix 247
- Canary Questions, 250
- Genchi Genbutsu 252
- First Principles 254
- Truth Translations 260
- Ad Blitz Razor 277
- Revenue Razor 277
- Stoic Surrender 285
- Silva Codebreaking 288
- Is This Asymmetrical? 300
- Metaphorical Lensing 280
- WADM 302
- Bayesian Thinking 306

Apathy | Depression, Beating
- RADAR 61
- Willpower Bootcamp 99
- North Star Offensive 102
- Theaters of War, Power 107
- Small Skirmishes 132
- Memory Alley 140
- Smallest Min Gain (SMG) 141
- Gratitude Goggles 149
- Embrace the Suck 151
- Life As 215
- Funk Buster 271
- Metaphorical Lensing 280
- Stoic Surrender 285

B
Business Opps, Evaluating
- Eventuality: Live in It's Skin 64
- Juggling a Zero (DARE) 78
- Force Multiplier 79
- Worst Case WARP Analysis 121
- Stop, Drop, and Roll 122
- Regret Rehearsal 130
- Then What? 131
- FICK 143
- Grounding Analogy 166
- Due Diligence 239
- Death is in the Details 243
- Canary Questions 250
- Genchi Genbutsu 252
- Edgelording 269
- Business in a Box Razor 277
- Expected Value 295
- Is This Asymmetrical 300
- WADM 302

C
Complexity, Gaining Clarity
- Force Multipliers 79
- North Star Offensive 102
- Tombstone Razors 277
- SCIRE 274
- DeMarco's Razor 277
- WADM 302
- Bayesian Thinking 306

Courage, Executing
- Worst Case WARP Analysis 121
- Phone Booth Persona 129
- WWJD 129
- Regret Rehearsal 130
- Then What? 131
- Small Skirmishes 132
- Pivot and Point 132
- FICK 143
- Unlimited Resources 170
- Do or Die 170
- "I am who I need to be" 172
- Buridan Butt Kick 282
- Stoic Surrender 285
- Is This Asymmetrical? 300

D

Debt, Elimination

- Eventuality: Live in Its Skin 64
- YODO 74
- Talk to the Shadow 136
- 90 Day War Game (Def) 137
- Identity Anchors 138
- Standing Orders 139
- Smallest Min Gain (SMG) 141
- Maestro Visualization 150
- Embrace the Suck 151
- Kaizen Chess 223
- Hansei 267
- SCIRE 274
- $600 Pizza Test 293

Deception, (Self or Others)

- RADAR 61
- The Gun+ $10M Question 104
- Grounding Analogy 166
- Attrition Doctrine 166
- Unlimited Resources 170
- Do or Die 170
- Zero-Based Thinking 171
- Truth Translations 260
- Revenue Razor, 277
- Metaphorical Lensing 280

Decision Clarity (High Risk)

- Slow the Moment 50
- Eventuality: Live in Its Skin 64
- Juggling a Zero 78
- Force Multiplier 79
- Worst Case WARP Analysis 121
- Regret Rehearsal 130
- Then What? 131
- Luck's Fortune/Death Decks 177
- Due Diligence 239
- Death is in the Details 243
- Rumsfeld Matrix 247
- Canary Questions 250
- Headline Razor 277
- Expected Value 295
- Is this Asymmetrical? 300
- WADM 302

Discipline, Executing

- Eventuality: Live in Its Skin 64
- Willpower Bootcamp 99
- Theaters of War, Power 107
- Talk to the Shadow 136
- 90 Day War Game (Off) 137
- Identity Anchors 139
- Standing Orders 139
- Memory Alley 140
- Smallest Min Gain (SMG) 141
- Hack the Kitchen 142
- Ten Turns 143
- Trigger Strategy 144
- Demosthenes 175
- Embrace the Suck 151
- Do or Die 170
- "I am who I need to be" 172
- Kaizen Chess 223
- 3As 309

Discomfort, Executing

- Willpower Bootcamp 99
- Gratitude Goggles 149
- Ten Turns 143
- Maestro Visualization 150
- Pain is Intel 150
- Embrace the Suck 151
- Do or Die 170
- Life As 215
- Backcasting 217
- Kaizen Chess 223
- Buridan Butt Kick 282

Divorce, Navigating

- Eventuality: Live in Its Skin 64
- WARP Worst Case Analysis 121
- Stop, Drop, and Roll 122
- WWJD 129
- Phone Booth Persona 129
- Then What? 131
- Zero-Based Thinking 171
- 1/2/3 Divorce Defense 257

E

Expectations, Adjusting

- Grounding Analogy 166
- Attrition Doctrine 166
- Scouts 167

F
Fear, Conquering
- North Star Offensive 102
- Worst Case WARP Analysis 121
- Phone Booth Persona 129
- WWJD 129
- Regret Rehearsal 130
- Then What? 131
- Small Skirmishes 132
- Point and Pivot 132
- FICK 143
- "I am who I need to be" 172
- Life As 215
- Backcasting 217
- Kaizen Chess 223
- Tombstone Razor, 277

Financial Opps, Evaluating
- Juggling a Zero (DARE) 78
- Force Multiplier 79
- Worst Case WARP Analysis 121
- Stop, Drop, and Roll 122
- Regret Rehearsal 130
- Then What? 131
- Due Diligence 239
- Death is in the Details 243
- Canary Questions 250
- Genchi Genbutsu 252
- Edgelording 269
- Revenue Razor 277
- Expected Value 295
- Is This Asymmetrical 300
- WADM 302

Focus, Improving
- Willpower Bootcamp 99
- North Star Offensive 102
- The Gun+ $10M Question 104
- Theaters of War, Power 107
- Hack the Kitchen 142
- Life As 215
- Backcasting 217
- Kaizen Chess 223
- Monkey First 312
- Atomic Domino 314
- Momentality Detox 317

H
Habits (Bad), Overcoming
Health, Improving
- Eventuality: Live in Its Skin 64
- Willpower Bootcamp 99
- North Star Offensive 102

- Talk to the Shadow 136
- 90 Day War Game (Off) 137
- Identity Anchors 138
- Standing Orders 139
- Memory Alley 140
- Smallest Min Gain (SMG) 141
- Hack the Kitchen 142
- Ten Turns 143
- Trigger Strategy 144
- Embrace the Suck 152
- Do or Die 170
- "I am who I need to be" 172
- Life As 215
- Backcasting 217
- Kaizen Chess 223
- Futurecasting 290
- Momentality Detox 317

I
Indecision, Overcoming
- Willpower Bootcamp 99
- North Star Offensive 102
- Phone Booth Persona 129
- WWJD 129
- Small Skirmishes 132
- Regret Rehearsal 130
- Buridan Butt Kick 282
- DeMarco's Razor 277
- Tombstone Razor 278
- Stoic Surrender 285

J
Job, Quitting
- Eventuality: Live in It's Skin 64
- Juggling a Zero (DARE) 78
- Force Multiplier 79
- Worst Case WARP Analysis 121
- Stop, Drop, and Roll 122
- Phone Booth Persona 129
- WWJD 129
- Regret Rehearsal 130
- Then What? 131
- FICK 143
- Luck's Fortune+Death Decks 177
- Life As 215
- Backcasting 217
- Kaizen Chess 223
- Hansei 267
- Edgelording 269
- Expected Value 295
- Is This Asymmetrical 300
- WADM 302

L
Laziness, Overcoming
- Eventuality: Live in Its Skin 64
- Willpower Bootcamp 99
- Northstar Offensive 102
- Talk to the Shadow 136
- 90 Day War Game (Off) 137
- Identity Anchors 138
- Standing Orders 139
- Memory Alley 140
- Smallest Min Gain (SMG) 141
- Hack the Kitchen 142
- Ten Turns 143
- Trigger Strategy 144
- Embrace the Suck 151
- Do or Die 170
- I am Who I Need to Be 172
- Life As 215
- Backcasting 217
- Kaizen Chess 223
- Futurecasting 290
- Momentality Detox 317

Luck, Improving
- Juggling a Zero 78
- Theaters of War, Power+Intel 107
- Luck's Fortune/Death Decks 177
- Directional Probability 183
- Poison Candy Gambit 185
- Due Diligence 239
- Rumsfeld Matrix 247
- Canary Questions 250
- Hansei 267

M
Marriage, Decisions Regarding
- Eventuality: Live in Its Skin 64
- WARP Worst Case Analysis 121
- Stop, Drop, and Roll 122
- WWJD 129
- Phone Booth Persona 129
- Then What? 131
- Zero-Based Thinking 171
- 1/2/3 Divorce Defense 257

N
New Frontiers, Taking
- Eventuality: Live in It's Skin 64
- Juggling a Zero (DARE) 78
- Force Multiplier 79
- Worst Case WARP Analysis 121
- Stop, Drop, and Roll 122
- Regret Rehearsal 130
- FICK 143
- Then What? 131
- Grounding Analogy 166
- Due Diligence 239
- Death is in the Details 243
- Canary Questions 250
- Genchi Genbutsu 252
- Edgelording 269
- Tombstone Razor 277
- Expected Value 295
- Is This Asymmetrical 300
- Stoic Surrender 285
- WADM 302

P
Past (Sabotage), Rewriting
- RADAR 61
- Big Ugly Funeral 63
- Willpower Bootcamp 99
- The Gun+ $10M Question 104
- Hansei 267

Perspective, Improving
- Willpower Bootcamp 99
- North Star Offensive 102
- Gratitude Googles 149
- Truth Translations 260
- Funk Buster 271
- Metaphorical Lensing 280

Problems, Solving
- First Principles 254
- SCIRE 274
- Silva Codebreaking 288
- WADM 302
- 3As 309
- Monkey First 312
- Atomic Domino 314

Project, Quitting
- Eventuality: Live in Its Skin 64
- WARP Worst Case Analysis 121
- Stop, Drop, and Roll 122
- WWJD 129
- Phone Booth Persona 129
- Then What? 131
- Zero-Based Thinking 171
- Hansei 267

Purchase Decisions (Big)
- Due Diligence 239
- Death is in the Details 243
- Rumsfeld Matrix 247
- Canary Questions 250
- Genchi Genbutsu 252
- First Principles (motives) 254
- $600 Pizza Test 293
- Expected Value 295
- Is this Asymmetrical 300
- WADM   302

R
Relationship, Ending
- Zero-Based Thinking 171
- Backcasting 217
- Kaizen Chess 223
- Life As 229
- Futurecasting 290
- Momentality Detox 317

R
Risk, Mitigating (Catastrophic)
- Slow the Moment 50
- Eventuality: Live in Its Skin 64
- Talk Some Sense to Him 68
- YODO 74
- Juggling a Zero 78
- Force Multiplier 79
- Worst Case WARP Analysis 121
- Regret Rehearsal 130
- Then What? 131
- Luck's Fortune/Death Decks 177
- Poison Candy Gambit 185
- Due Diligence 239
- Death is in the Details 243
- Rumsfeld Matrix 247
- Canary Questions 250
- Is this Asymmetrical? 300

S
Skill Acquisition
- North Star Offensive 102
- Small Skirmishes 132
- 90 Day War Game (Off) 137
- Smallest Min Gain (SMG) 141
- Demosthenes 175
- Life As 215
- Backcasting 217
- Kaizen Chess 223
- 3As 309

Stress, Mitigation
- Gratitude Googles 149
- Funk Buster 271
- Tombstone Razor 278
- Stoic Surrender 285

T
Time, Finding
- Willpower Bootcamp 99
- North Star Offensive 102
- The Gun+ $10M Question 104
- Theaters of War, Power 107
- Hack the Kitchen 142
- Life As 215
- Backcasting 217
- Kaizen Chess 223
- Monkey First 312
- Atomic Domino 314
- Momentality Detox 317

W
Wealth Building
- Eventuality: Live in It's Skin 64
- Force Multiplier 79
- Regret Rehearsal 130
- Phone Booth Persona 129
- WWJD 129
- Smallest Min Gain (SMG) 141
- Maestro Visualization 150
- Grounding Analogy 166
- Life As 215
- Backcasting 217
- Kaizen Chess 223
- Futurecasting 290
- 3As 309

Appendix C
Choose Hard, Live Easy Cheat Sheets

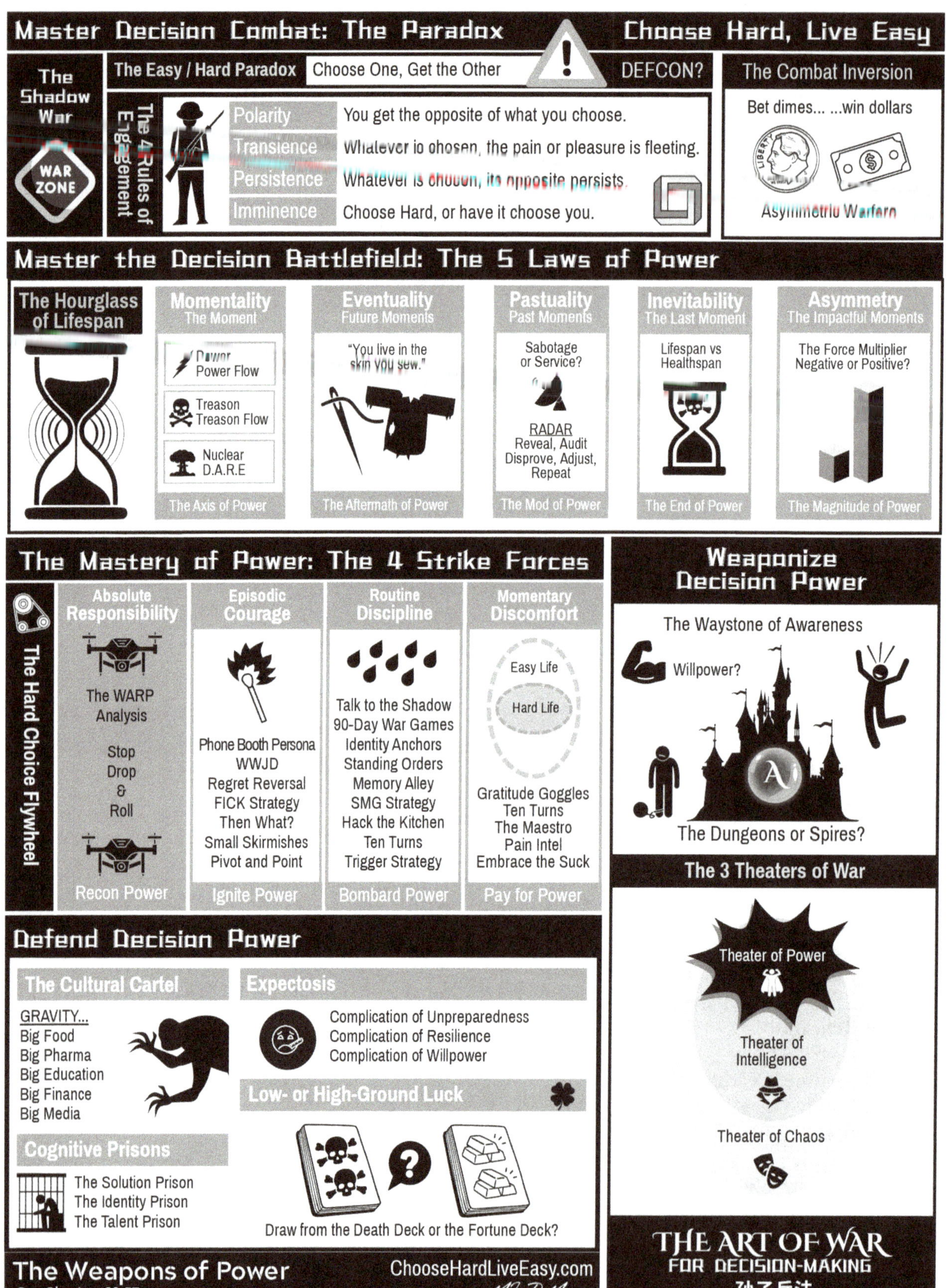

 Strategizing the War: Lifelong Decision Battleplans

BACKCASTING
The Focus of Power

KAIZEN CHESS
The Sharing of Power

"LIFE AS"...
The Alchemy of Power

Reverse Engineer Your Future
"Best You"

The Royal Guard of Happiness
"Best You"

Misery Militia
"Worst You"

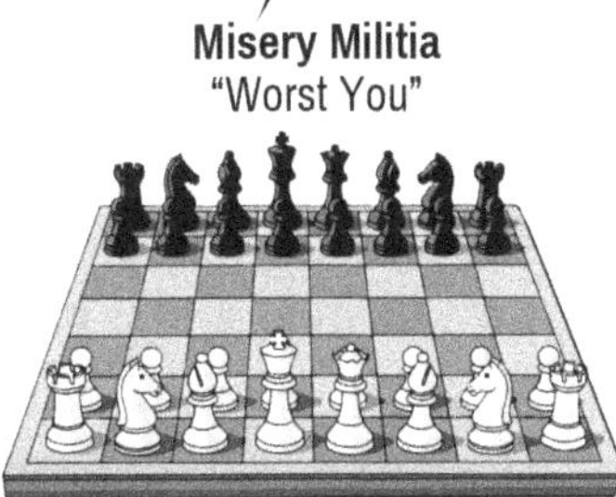

Deploy as Determined by Objective

Life As a Video Game
Optimize Discipline, Growth, Willpower

Life As a Movie
Optimize Courage, Discomfort, Willpower

Life As a CEO
Optimize Responsibility, Efficiency, Balance

⚔ The Decision Armory
Clear the Fog of War, Win the Moment, Win the Day, and Win Life

⚖ Weapons of Truth and Intelligence

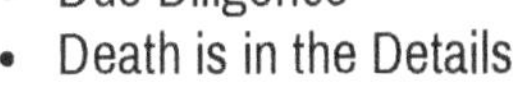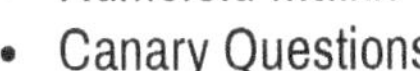

- Due Diligence
- Death is in the Details
- Rumsfeld Matrix
- Canary Questions
- Genchi Genbutsu

- First Principles
- 1/2/3 Divorce Defense
- Truth Translations
- Hansei
- Pedantic Edgelording

Weapons of Reason and Strategy

- The Funk Buster
- The SCIRE Framework
- Metaphorical Lensing
- The Buridan Buttkick
- Stoic Surrender
- The Silva Codebreaker
- Futurecasting

Thinking Razors

- DeMarco's Razor
- The Sellout Razor
- The Tombstone Razor
- The "Business in a Box" Razor
- The Revenue Razor

🔓 Weapons of Decryption

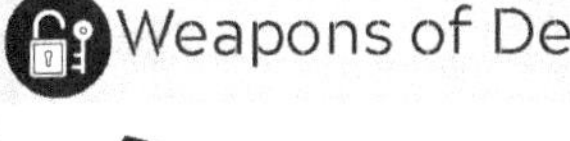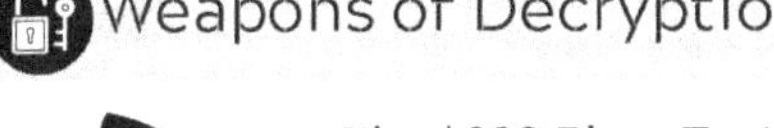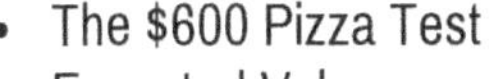

- The $600 Pizza Test
- Expected Value
- Is This Asymmetrical?
- WADM
- Bayesian

💥 Weapons of Engagement

- The 3A Strategy
- The Monkey First Strategy
- The Atomic Domino Strategy
- The Momentality Detox

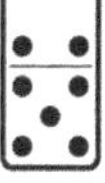

The Decision Battlefield
See Chapters 1-28

ChooseHardLiveEasy.com
MJ DeMarco

THE ART OF WAR
FOR DECISION-MAKING
—— 孙子兵法 ——

The Axis of Power or Weakness

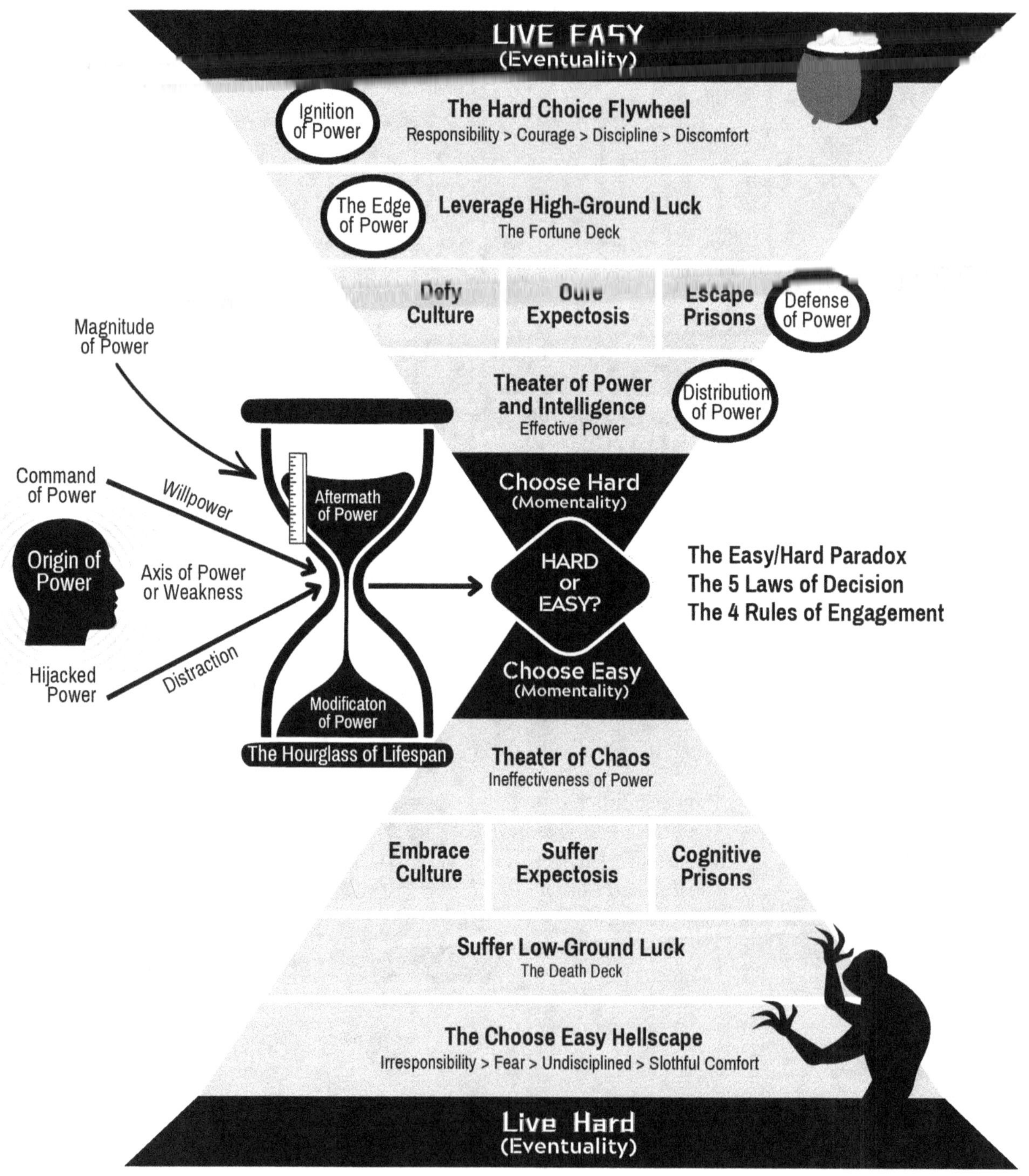

Appendix D
W.A.D.M. Worksheets

Triage a complex decision. The Weighted Average Decision Matrix examines several decisions through a subjective analysis of values and factors multiplied by their importance. Those are values are summed to arrive at a definitive decision based on the higher number.

		Decision Option A Example: Move to Ohio	Decision Option B Example: Stay in NYC
FACTORS AND VALUES	**FACTOR WEIGHT (1-10)**	**DECISION A**	**DECISION B**
	TOTALS ...		

WADM WORKSHEET

Triage a complex decision. The Weighted Average Decision Matrix examines several decisions through a subjective analysis of factors and values multiplied by their importance. Those are values are summed to arrive at a definitive decision based on the higher number.

		Decision Option A Example: Move to Ohio	Decision Option B Example: Stay in NYC
FACTORS AND VALUES	FACTOR WEIGHT (1-10)	DECISION A	DECISION B
	TOTALS …		

WADM WORKSHEET

Triage a complex decision. The Weighted Average Decision Matrix examines several decisions through a subjective analysis of factors and values multiplied by their importance. Those are values are summed to arrive at a definitive decision based on the higher number.

		Decision Option A Example: Move to Ohio	Decision Option B Example: Stay in NYC
FACTORS AND VALUES	FACTOR WEIGHT (1-10)	DECISION A	DECISION B
	TOTALS ...		

Appendix E
Kaizen Chess Scorecards

Kaizen Chess is the tactical pursuit of compounding daily happiness across its five proven pillars. The board resets every morning. On one side, the Misery Militia fights to drag you toward your worst life; on the other, the Royal Guard of Happiness creates your best. Every 24 hours is a fresh firefight, and the side that scores the most points by midnight wins the war for the day. The goal is simple: Be better today than you were yesterday. Accomplish this often, and Live Easy awaits.

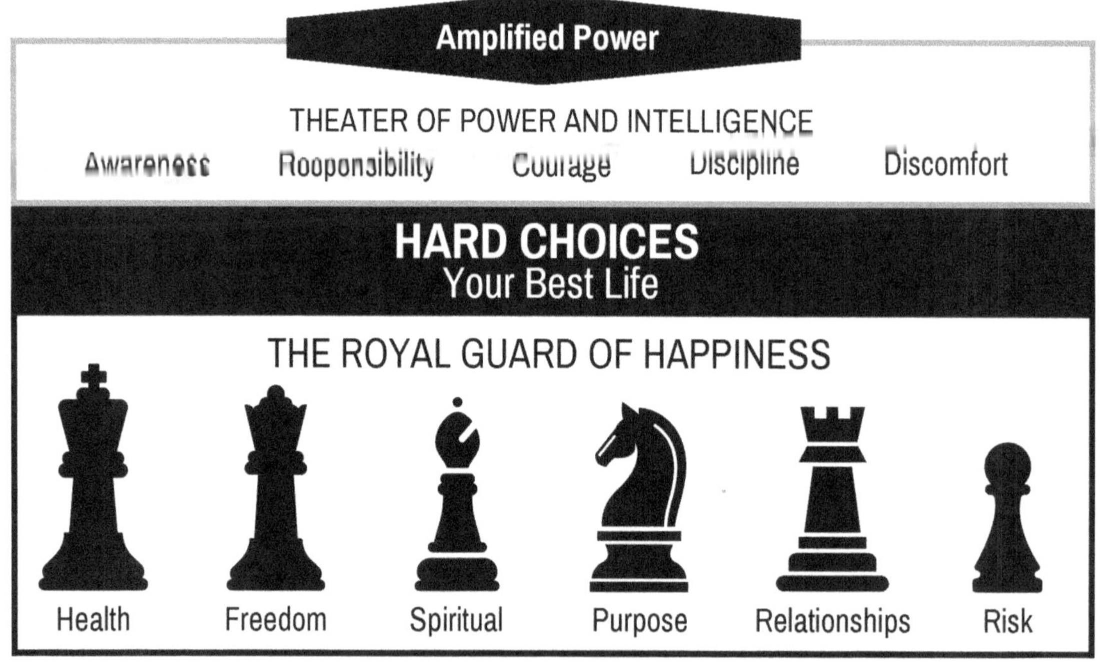

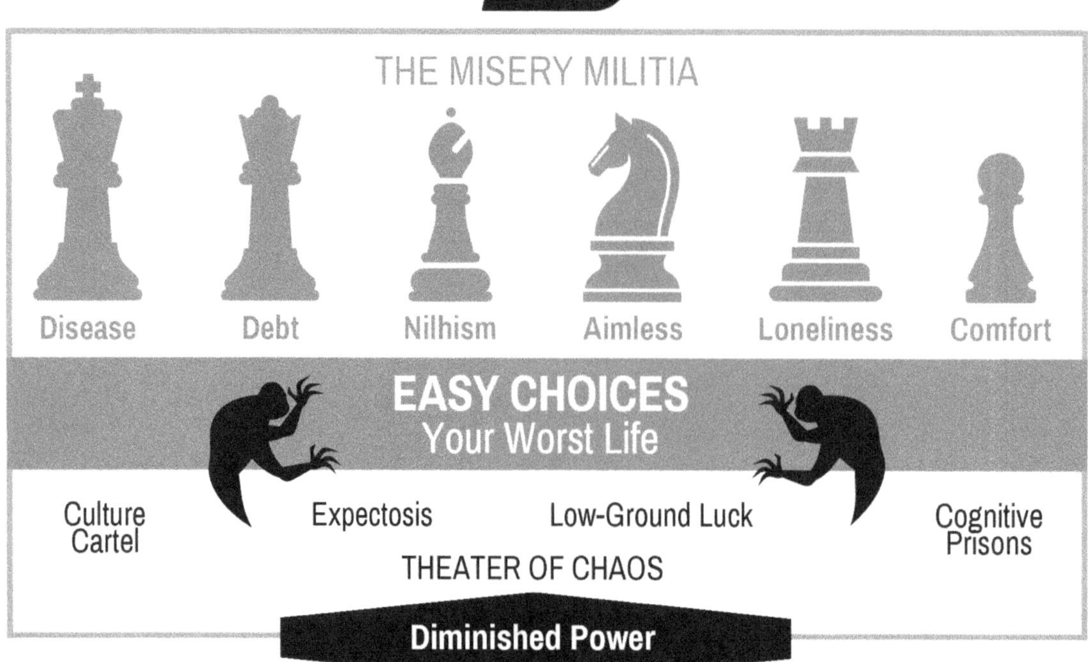

Kaizen Chess

DATE ____________________

Happiness Factor	Kaizen Wins (Hard) Moments Won	Decision Debts (Easy) Moments Lost	Net
Health			
Freedom			
Spiritual			
Purpose			
Relationships			
Risk			
TOTALS	Total Moments Won	Total Moments Lost	Net

VICTORY!   DEFEAT!   Positive number = You won the day!
Negative number = You lost the day!

Kaizen Chess

DATE ______________________

Happiness Factor	Kaizen Wins (Hard) Moments Won	Decision Debts (Easy) Moments Lost	Net
♚ Health			
♛ Freedom			
♝ Spiritual			
♞ Purpose			
♜ Relationships			
♟ Risk			
TOTALS	Total Moments Won	Total Moments Lost	Net

VICTORY! 　DEFEAT! 　Positive number = You won the day!
Negative number = You lost the day!

Kaizen Chess

DATE ____________________

Happiness Factor	Kaizen Wins (Hard) Moments Won	Decision Debts (Easy) Moments Lost	Net
♔ Health			
♕ Freedom			
♗ Spiritual			
♘ Purpose			
♖ Relationships			
♙ Risk			
TOTALS	Total Moments Won	Total Moments Lost	Net

VICTORY!    DEFEAT!

Positive number = You won the day!
Negative number = You lost the day!

Appendix F
Weaponizing Awareness, Exercising Willpower

Silicon Valley has turned your brain into a slot machine. If you aren't pissed off about this, you're an addict denying your addiction. But the solution isn't to smash your phone or move to a monastery. The solution is to fight back using the exact weapon the culture has trained you to abandon: *Willpower*.

Right now, an army of feel-good gurus is trying to convince you that willpower is a fool's errand. They tell you it's "unreliable." They tell you to "follow your passion" instead.

This is a trap. Passion is a fair-weather friend. It's great when the sun is shining, but the second the work gets Hard, passion packs its rainbow-colored bags and leaves you stranded.

What gets the roof built in the pouring rain is the gritty, unglamorous, and utterly essential force of *will*.

Of course your willpower feels unreliable right now. It's as weak as a wet paper bag because you've never trained it. Expecting it to save you in a crisis is like trying to bench press 300 pounds when you can barely lift a case of beer.

Vilifying willpower is just another invitation to dose a new strain of Easy.

Willpower is simply the conscious command of your Awareness in the present moment. It is a muscle. It isn't gone; it has just been benched by Team Twitch, Team Zuckerberg, and Team TikTok.

The 12-Day Willpower Bootcamp is a progressive overload program for your brain. Like any muscle, willpower is built through incremental, consistent tension. You will start small, rack up micro-wins, and forge the strength required to command your own life.

Anytime you want to get willpower in the gym and transform it into a reliable, power-flexing muscle, execute the 12-day bootcamp. Why bother?

Because willpower is the driver of Awareness. And Awareness is the nuts and bolts of all decision.

The 12-Day Willpower Bootcamp

Exercise and Strengthen Willpower — Reclaim Awareness

Win a Simple Battle (Day 1 - 12) Make your bed for 12 days

| Day 1 | 2 | 3 | 4 | 5 | 6 | 7 | 8 | 9 | 10 | 11 | 12 |

Become a Finisher (Day 2 - 12) Finish what you start

| Day 2 | 3 | 4 | 5 | 6 | 7 | 8 | 9 | 10 | 11 | 12 |

Defeat Notifications (Day 3-12) Disable all non-essential notifications

| Day 3 | 4 | 5 | 6 | 7 | 8 | 9 | 10 | 11 | 12 |

Resieze Awareness (Day 4-12) Push-ups or knee bends every hour

| Day 4 | 5 | 6 | 7 | 8 | 9 | 10 | 11 | 12 |

Kill Multitasking Focus only on one task at a time

| Day 5 | 6 | 7 | 8 | 9 | 10 | 11 | 12 |

Breath in the Silence Sit in silence for 5 minutes while counting breaths to 10 repeatedly

| Day 6 | 7 | 8 | 9 | 10 | 11 | 12 |

Trigger a New Story Re-narrate all ambushed awareness

| Day 7 | 8 | 9 | 10 | 11 | 12 |

Direct the Silence Direct the silence

| Day 8 | 9 | 10 | 11 | 12 |

Go the Extra Mile Do more and better in every task

| Day 9 | 10 | 11 | 12 |

The Gauntlet Turn your smartphone into a dumbphone—only essentials

| DAY 10 | DAY 11 | DAY 12 |

VICTORY!   DEFEAT!

The 12-Day Willpower Bootcamp

Exercise and Strengthen Willpower — Reclaim Awareness

Win a Simple Battle (Day 1 - 12) Make your bed for 12 days

| Day 1 | 2 | 3 | 4 | 5 | 6 | 7 | 0 | 9 | 10 | 11 | 12 |

Become a Finisher (Day 2 - 12) Finish what you start

| Day 2 | 3 | 4 | 5 | 6 | 7 | 8 | 9 | 10 | 11 | 12 |

Defeat Notifications (Day 3-12) Disable all non-essential notifications

| Day 3 | 4 | 5 | 6 | 7 | 8 | 9 | 10 | 11 | 12 |

Resieze Awareness (Day 4-12) Push-ups or knee bends every hour

| Day 4 | 5 | 6 | 7 | 8 | 9 | 10 | 11 | 12 |

Kill Multitasking Focus only on one task at a time

| Day 5 | 6 | 7 | 8 | 9 | 10 | 11 | 12 |

Breath in the Silence Sit in silence for 5 minutes while counting breaths to 10 repeatedly

| Day 6 | 7 | 8 | 9 | 10 | 11 | 12 |

Trigger a New Story Re-narrate all ambushed awareness

| Day 7 | 8 | 9 | 10 | 11 | 12 |

Direct the Silence Direct the silence

| Day 8 | 9 | 10 | 11 | 12 |

Go the Extra Mile Do more and better in every task

| Day 9 | 10 | 11 | 12 |

The Gauntlet Turn your smartphone into a dumbphone—only essentials

| DAY 10 | DAY 11 | DAY 12 |

VICTORY!   DEFEAT!

The 12-Day Willpower Bootcamp

Exercise and Strengthen Willpower — Reclaim Awareness

Win a Simple Battle (Day 1 - 12) Make your bed for 12 days

| Day 1 | 2 | 3 | 4 | 5 | 6 | 7 | 8 | 9 | 10 | 11 | 12 |

Become a Finisher (Day 2 - 12) Finish what you start

| Day 2 | 3 | 4 | 5 | 6 | 7 | 8 | 9 | 10 | 11 | 12 |

Defeat Notifications (Day 3-12) Disable all non-essential notifications

| Day 3 | 4 | 5 | 6 | 7 | 8 | 9 | 10 | 11 | 12 |

Resieze Awareness (Day 4-12) Push-ups or knee bends every hour

| Day 4 | 5 | 6 | 7 | 8 | 9 | 10 | 11 | 12 |

Kill Multitasking Focus only on one task at a time

| Day 5 | 6 | 7 | 8 | 9 | 10 | 11 | 12 |

Breath in the Silence Sit in silence for 5 minutes while counting breaths to 10 repeatedly

| Day 6 | 7 | 8 | 9 | 10 | 11 | 12 |

Trigger a New Story Re-narrate all ambushed awareness

| Day 7 | 8 | 9 | 10 | 11 | 12 |

Direct the Silence Direct the silence

| Day 8 | 9 | 10 | 11 | 12 |

Go the Extra Mile Do more and better in every task

| Day 9 | 10 | 11 | 12 |

The Gauntlet Turn your smartphone into a dumbphone—only essentials

| DAY 10 | DAY 11 | DAY 12 |

VICTORY!   DEFEAT!

Appendix G
Backcasting "To Do" Lists

The strategy is brilliantly beautiful. You plant your flag on an ambitious 10-year moonshot, then reverse-engineer the ascent into a triad of milestones—5 years, 1 year, monthly, and finally, the Weekly Mission. This weaponizes your time, transforming insurmountable mountains into actionable molehills. By focusing all your Power on a single weekly objective, you turn *Someday* fantasies into immediate, tactical strikes that bridge the gap between today's reality and tomorrow's empire.

Success is never stumbled upon as a lottery Event; it is forged through a relentless Process. You can't predict every pothole or pivot, but Backcasting forces you to be the architect of your own destiny instead of letting culture draft your blueprints (which usually culminate in a cubicle and a mortgage you hate). The momentum is born in the trenches, executing the work right in front of your face, one week at a time. And the ultimate payoff? Even if the fog of war pushes you off your exact coordinates, the trajectory alone guarantees you'll land somewhere spectacular. Live Easy awaits.

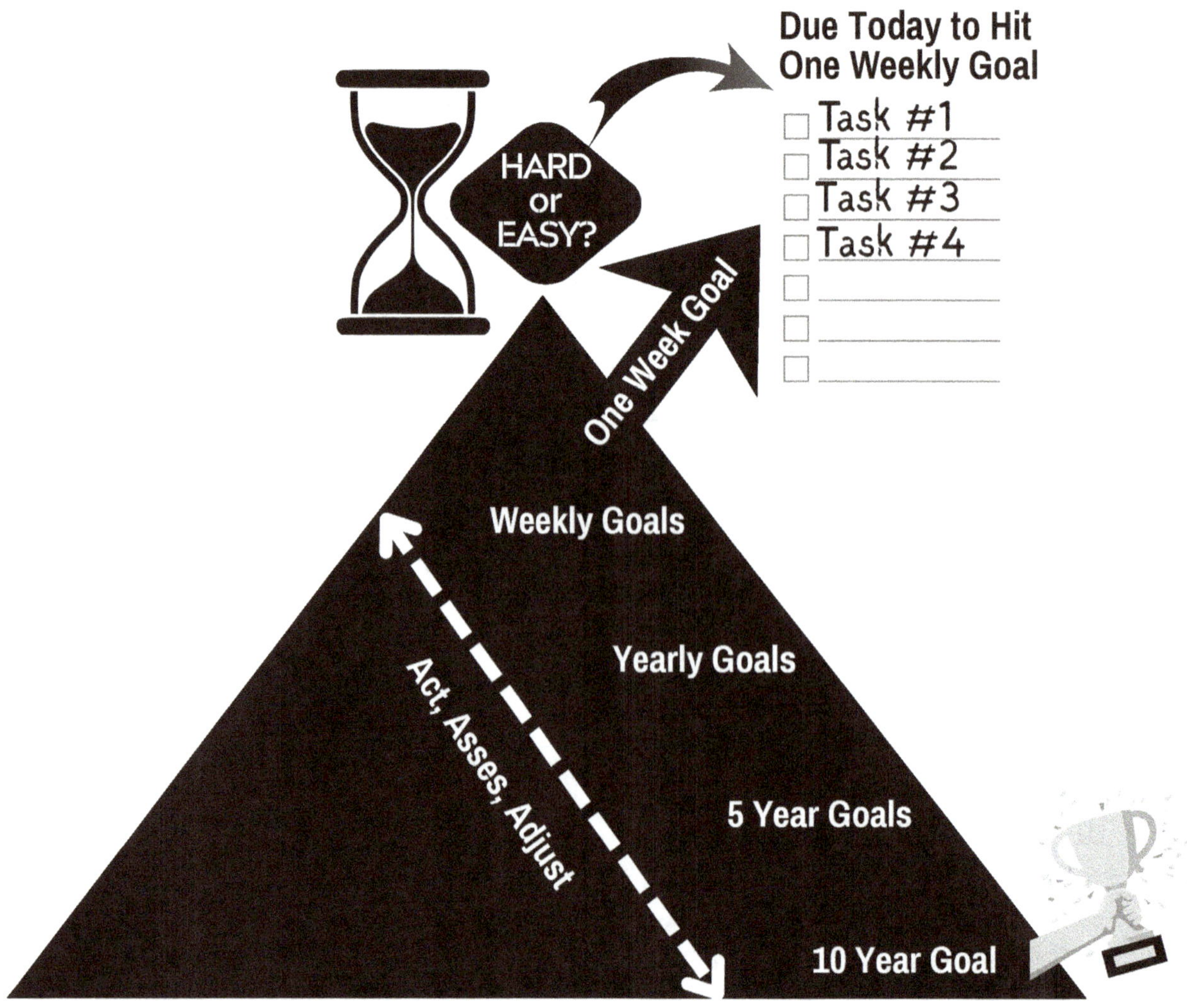

DATE:

TOTAL POINTS:

🎯 BEST-LIFE ENGINEERING

< 30 (Day Off?)	30-39 (Fair)	40-49 (Challenger!)	50+ (Warrior!)	80+ (Goal Ninja!)

☑ MY ATOMIC DOMINO (POWER TASK) [50 points for completion]
What is the the most important action you need to accomplish today, optimally a task that moves you closer to stated goals?

1

Weekly Goals

Before the week, write down your weekly goals that will directly influence the **MONTHLY** goal.

☑ MY PRIMARY TASKS TODAY [5 points each completion]
What are the urgent and/or important actions you need to accomplish today, optimally a task that moves you closer to stated goals?

1
2
3
4
5
6
7
8
9
10
11
12
13
14
15

Monthly Goals

Before the week, write down your monthly goals that will directly influence the **YEARLY** goal.

One Year Goals

Every few weeks, write down your goals for the year that will directly influence the **FIVE YEAR** goals.

☑ MY SECONDARY TASKS TO CONSIDER [2 points each completion]
What tasks should you potentially address that aren't necessarily important or urgent?

1
2
3
4
5

Five Year Goals

Periodically envision & record your five year goals that will influence your **TEN YEAR** dream life.

➤ REMINDERS FOR TOMORROW OR WEEKEND
Add any tasks or reminders here that you did not finish, or could be addressed potentially tomorrow or on the weekend.

1
2
3

Ten Year Dream Life

Periodically envision & write your ten year goals that frame your **OPTIMUM DREAM LIFE.**

"The same habits of the old year will get you the same results of the new year. Change something, or change nothing."
M.J DeMarco, Entrepreneur and Author of The Millionaire Fastlane

☼ **DATE:** ☼ ☼ **TOTAL POINTS:** ☼

| < 30 (Day Off?) | 30-39 (Fair) | 40-49 (Challenger!) | 50+ (Warrior!) | 80+ (Goal Ninja!) |

☑ **MY ATOMIC DOMINO (POWER TASK)** [50 points for completion]
What is the the most important action you need to accomplish today, optimally a task that moves you closer to stated goals?

1 ____ DONE

☑ **MY PRIMARY TASKS TODAY** [5 points each completion]
What are the urgent and/or important actions you need to accomplish today, optimally a task that moves you closer to stated goals?

1 ____ DONE
2 ____ DONE
3 ____ DONE
4 ____ DONE
5 ____ DONE
6 ____ DONE
7 ____ DONE
8 ____ DONE
9 ____ DONE
10 ____ DONE
11 ____ DONE
12 ____ DONE
13 ____ DONE
14 ____ DONE
15 ____ DONE

☑ **MY SECONDARY TASKS TO CONSIDER** [2 points each completion]
What tasks should you potentially address that aren't necessarily important or urgent?

1 ____ DONE
2 ____ DONE
3 ____ DONE
4 ____ DONE
5 ____ DONE

⊙ **REMINDERS FOR TOMORROW OR WEEKEND**
Add any tasks or reminders here that you did not finish, or could be addressed potentially tomorrow or on the weekend.

1 ____
2 ____
3 ____

⊘ BEST-LIFE ENGINEERING

Weekly Goals

Before the week, write down your weekly goals that will directly influence the **MONTHLY** goal.

Monthly Goals

Before the week, write down your monthly goals that will directly influence the **YEARLY** goal.

One Year Goals

Every few weeks, write down your goals for the year that will directly influence the **FIVE YEAR** goals.

Five Year Goals

Periodically envision & record your five year goals that will influence your **TEN YEAR** dream life.

Ten Year Dream Life

Periodically envision & write your ten year goals that frame your **OPTIMUM DREAM LIFE.**

"The same habits of the old year will get you the same results of the new year. Change something, or change nothing."
MJ DeMarco, Entrepreneur and Author of The Millionaire Fastlane

✿ **DATE:** ✿ ✿ **TOTAL POINTS:** ✿

| < 30 (Day Off?) | 30-39 (Fair) | 40-49 (Challenger!) | 50+ (Warrior!) | 80+ (Goal Ninja!) |

☑ MY ATOMIC DOMINO (POWER TASK) [50 points for completion]

What is the the most important action you need to accomplish today, optimally a task that moves you closer to stated goals?

1

☑ MY PRIMARY TASKS TODAY [5 points each completion]

What are the urgent and/or important actions you need to accomplish today, optimally a task that moves you closer to stated goals?

1
2
3
4
5
6
7
8
9
10
11
12
13
14
15

☑ MY SECONDARY TASKS TO CONSIDER [2 points each completion]

What tasks should you potentially address that aren't necessarily important or urgent?

1
2
3
4
5

➥ REMINDERS FOR TOMORROW OR WEEKEND

Add any tasks or reminders here that you did not finish, or could be addressed potentially tomorrow or on the weekend.

1
2
3

⊘ BEST-LIFE ENGINEERING

Weekly Goals ⚙

Before the week, write down your weekly goals that will directly influence the **MONTHLY** goal.

Monthly Goals ⚙

Before the week, write down your monthly goals that will directly influence the **YEARLY** goal.

One Year Goals ⚙

Every few weeks, write down your goals for the year that will directly influence the **FIVE YEAR** goals.

Five Year Goals ⚙

Periodically envision & record your five year goals that will influence your **TEN YEAR** dream life.

Ten Year Dream Life ⚙

Periodically envision & write your ten year goals that frame your **OPTIMUM DREAM LIFE.**

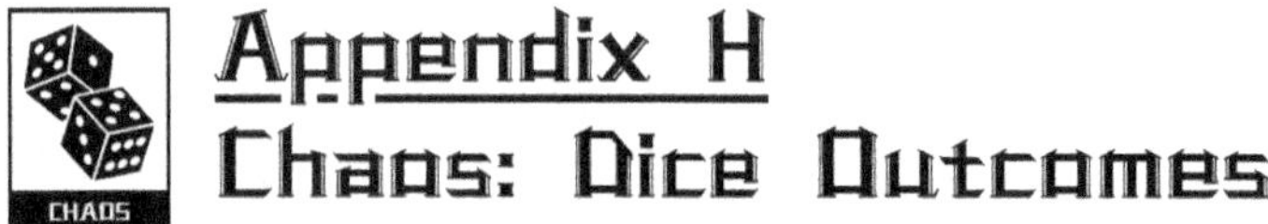

Appendix H
Chaos: Dice Outcomes

#1–THE DECISION GAUNTLET

Ghost Pepper: You played the practical joke.
ROLL 2 or 3—The Felony Roll
He has an undiagnosed ulcer or a severe allergic reaction.
An ambulance is called. Security footage catches you.
You're fired for assault with a dangerous substance and face
a lawsuit that drains your bank account.
ROLL 4, 5, or 6—The HR Meat-Grinder
He realizes immediately it was tampered with. You're
hauled into HR for workplace harassment. You lose your
bonus, get a permanent mark on your record, and become
the office psycho no one wants to promote.
ROLL 7—The Friendly Fire
He realizes the burrito is spicy and offers a bite to your
boss. You watch in horror as you accidentally poison the
person who signs your checks.
ROLL 8, 9 or 10—The Escalation War
He knows it was you. Instead of stopping, he views this as
an invitation to a Prank War. Now you have to worry
about laxatives in your coffee or your car being keyed. Your
peace of mind is officially dead.
ROLL 11 or 12—The Hollow Win
He gets burned, figures out the joke, and stops. You get
away with it.

Ghost Pepper: You did nothing.
ROLL 2, 3, 4, 5, 6 or 7—The Boredom
Because you ignored him, his petty pranks stop.
ROLL 8, 9, or 10—The Friend
You laugh and congratulate him for well played pranks.
You end up great friends.
ROLL 11 or 12—The HR Play
You confront him and warn him that you will report him
to HR. His behavior stops immediately.

The Flirty Neighbor: You accept the sexual tryst.
ROLL 2 or 3—Instant Implosion
Her husband walks in. It turns violent or leads to an
immediate, public, life-shattering divorce. You lose the
house, the kids, and 50% of everything before the BBQ
coals are even cold.
ROLL 4, 5, 6 or 7—The Gossip Grenade
She's a leaker. Within 48 hours, the secret is neighborhood
currency. Your wife finds out through a "concerned" text
from a friend. The social shunning begins; you are the
neighborhood predator.
ROLL 8, 9 or 10—The Slow Poison
You get away with it, but the rot starts from within. You
can't look at your kids without feeling like a fraud. You
distance yourself from your wife to manage the guilt, and
the marriage dies a slow death over the next 5 years.
ROLL 11 or 12—The Phantom Win
You get away clean. No one knows. But you've just
rewritten your internal code as a douchebag, hunting for
the next hit. You'll roll again soon, and the curve always
eventually hits a 2.

The Flirty Neighbor: You did nothing, politely declined.
ROLL 2, 3, 4, 5, 6 or 7—The Good Dad
You walk back to the grill, hand your wife a drink, and ruffle
your kids' hair. No one knows what happened. You carry the
secret as a badge of honor and a victory in the shadow war.
ROLL 8, 9, or 10—The Full Disclosure
You tell your wife exactly what happened. The honesty
creates a bonding effect, and it strengthens. You both realize
this neighborhood isn't your tribe. You start looking for a
better kingdom
ROLL 12—The Bunny Boiler
She feels rejected and dangerous. She tells her husband you
propositioned her. It's a week of hell and drama, but because
your decision-making and integrity is spotless, your wife and
the neighborhood believe you.

Benevolent Parents: You bought your kid a Toyota.
ROLL 2 or 3—The Workhorse Tax
Because he has a truck, he becomes the unpaid mover for
everyone in his class. He's constantly hauling furniture and
gear for friends, which actually teaches him the value of
service and hard work.
ROLL 4, 5, 6, or 7—The Caretaker
He thanks you for the new truck after learning how
expensive they are. He learns to appreciate the gift and takes
care of the truck as if it bought it himself.
ROLL 8, 9 or 10—The Side Hustle
He starts a side-hustle hauling mulch or junk, making his
own money. He builds a personality that doesn't rely on a
silver spoon V8.
ROLL 11 or 12—The Unified Front
Your wife feels respected and heard. Your marriage hits a new
level of synchronicity because you chose the big picture over
your personal high school baggage. The son thrives because
his parents are a boss team.

Benevolent Parents: You bought your kid a Corvette.
ROLL 2 or 3—The Total Loss
450 horsepower meets a wet road and a TikTok pull. The car
is wrapped around a tree within a month. Your son is killed,
and you're buried in guilt, grief, and a soon to be dead
marriage.
ROLL 4, 5, or 6—The Narcissist Seed
He becomes the neighborhood rich kid. His popularity is
based on the car, not character. He stops working hard
because he's already peaked at 17, destroying his drive to
build his own Fastlane.
ROLL 7—The Maintenance Pit
Insurance premiums for a teen in a 'Vette are a second
mortgage. Between the tickets and the Easy life ego, he views
you as an ATM rather than a mentor.
ROLL 8, 9 or 10—The Marital Fracture
You overruled your wife's practical (and correct) intuition.
Every time the car gets a scratch or your son acts entitled, it's
a "told you so" hand grenade in your marriage.
ROLL 11 or 12—The Unicorn
He respects the machine, handles the fame with grace, and
becomes the coolest kid in school. You feel validated, but
you've effectively spoiled his hunger for future struggle.

#2– OUTCOME: THE INVISIBLE WITNESS

Below, look up the score you gave yourself from Part 1 (How would MJ rate what he witnessed?) and then roll your dice. Examine the potential outcomes (A - E) for your future based on the number you rolled.

Rating (1-3)
- Roll 2 or 12: Outcome B
- Roll 3 or 4: Outcome C
- Roll 5 or 6: Outcome D
- Roll 7 or 8 or 9: Outcome D
- Roll 10 or 11: Outcome E

Rating (7-8)
- Roll 2 or 12: Outcome E
- Roll 3 or 4: Outcome D
- Roll 5 or 6: Outcome C
- Roll 7 to 8 or 9: Outcome B
- Roll 10 or 11: Outcome A

Rating (4-6)
- Roll 2 or 12: Outcome A
- Roll 3 or 4: Outcome B
- Roll 5 or 6: Outcome C
- Roll 7 or 8 or 9: Outcome D
- Roll 10 or 11: Outcome E

Rating (9-10)
- Roll 2 or 12: Outcome D
- Roll 3 or 4: Outcome C
- Roll 5 or 6: Outcome B
- Roll 7 or 8 or 9: Outcome A
- Roll 10 or 11: Outcome B

#3– OUTCOME: DEFCON / DECISIONAL FALLOUT SCORE

Examine your Decisional Fallout Score (DFS) from Chapter 5. Roll your dice, live and feel the outcome (A-E, bottom).

DEFCON (≤ 60)
- Roll 2 or 12: Outcome B
- Roll 3 or 4: Outcome C
- Roll 5 or 6: Outcome D
- Roll 7 or 8 or 9: Outcome D
- Roll 10 or 11: Outcome E

DEFCON 84, 80, 76
- Roll 2 or 12: Outcome E
- Roll 3 or 4: Outcome D
- Roll 5 or 6: Outcome C
- Roll 7 to 8 or 9: Outcome B
- Roll 10 or 11: Outcome A

DEFCON 72, 68, 64, 60
- Roll 2 or 12: Outcome A
- Roll 3 or 4: Outcome B
- Roll 5 or 6: Outcome C
- Roll 7 or 8 or 9: Outcome D
- Roll 10 or 11: Outcome E

DEFCON 100, 96, 92, 88
- Roll 2 or 12: Outcome D
- Roll 3 or 4: Outcome C
- Roll 5 or 6: Outcome B
- Roll 7 or 8 or 9: Outcome A
- Roll 10 or 11: Outcome B

A-THE ARCHITECT (The 5%) You Chose Hard, and you built the fortress. You achieved total financial and time autonomy. You dictate your schedule, your health is optimized, and your legacy is secure. You didn't just survive the war; you conquered it, earning a lifetime of Easy.

B-THE GOLDEN HANDCUFFS (The Comfortable Compromise) You fought enough skirmishes to secure comfort, but you ultimately surrendered to the Safe path (Big Education / Big Finance). You have a nice house, a decent car, and a 401k, but you spent 40 years building someone else's empire. It's a decent life, but it ends with a lingering, haunting whisper of "What if I had taken the shot?"

C-THE NPC BASELINE (The Muddy Middle) You didn't crash and burn, but you never took off. You represent the 5.5 on the Cantril Scale. You paid your bills, worked a job you tolerated, watched 10,000 hours of television, and died quietly. You survived the game, but you never actually played it. Your tombstone should read: "He did nothing memorable."

D-THE SLOW BLEED (Quiet Desperation) You surrendered to the minor, daily Easy choices. Now you're trapped in the paycheck-to-paycheck cycle. Your health is a low-level chronic ache, your marriage is basically a roommate agreement, and your credit card debt dictates your future. You are a low-level, exhausted battery powering the Cultural Cartel.

E-THE CARTEL CASUALTY (The Default Reality) You swallowed the propaganda and embraced the Cult of Easy. You bought the car you couldn't afford, ate the garbage they advertised, and surrendered your Awareness to the screen. Eventuality arrived with a wrecking ball: bankrupt, divorced, and medically dependent on Big Pharma. Shadow War, lost.

#4– OUTCOME: THE PASTOR IN THE PARKING LOT

Your wife didn't Stop, Drop, and Roll. She posted the video. Here are the outcomes.

ROLL 2—THE CREEP

The pastor was a regular getting lap dances and other whatever else happens "behind the curtain". You are the hero for the hour and the pastor is fired, but now the scandal has tainted the church. A third of the congregation leaves.

ROLL 3—THE ADDICT

The pastor has a gambling addiction and was meeting a loan shark at the club. He is fired and spirals. You are now the snitch who kicks people when they are down.

ROLL 4 or 5 —THE RESEARCHER

The pastor claims he was "doing research on sin" for a sermon. He was actually interviewing a variety of customers and dancers. A messy, ambiguous public debate ensues. Half the town hates you for judging him; the other half thinks he's lying.

ROLL 6 or 8— THE SUICIDE INTERVENTION

A dancer (a former youth group member) texted him saying she was going to end her life. He rushed over to talk her down. You just publicly shamed a man while he was saving a human life. You are the villain of the year.

ROLL 9 or 10— THE RUNAWAY DAUGHTER

A parishioner called him in a panic—his teenage daughter (a minor) was spotted there dancing. The Pastor went in to drag her out and confront the ownership. The father posts a video crying, thanking the Pastor. You look like a judgmental monster. The Pastor sues you for defamation. You lose everything.

ROLL 11—THE SIDE HUSTLE

The church pays him poverty wages. He is a licensed plumber on the side and was there to fix a clogged toilet so he can feed his kids. You just mocked a working father for trying to provide for his family. The internet turns on you instantly.

ROLL 12— THE DIABETIC

The pastor was delivering emergency insulin to a diabetic church member who works the day shift there as a server and forgot her bag. The "Stripper" posts a photo of her insulin pump and her basic waitstaff uniform. You are labeled a Pharisee and a bully. You leave the church because everyone hates you and your wife.

#5–OUTCOMES: XMAS AT THE COFFEE SHOP

You chose Easy. You left your $80,000 tote bag with a stranger to save your precious table. Roll two dice to see if the Universe punishes your laziness or enables your bad habits and Death Deck draws.

ROLL 2— TOTAL WIPEOUT

The Nightmare Scenario. You return to find the chair empty. The grandmotherly woman was part of a professional theft ring targeting holiday shoppers. Car stolen. Laptop stolen. Bank accounts drained. You are stranded without a phone or coat in December. You bet your life on a smile, and you lost everything. Welcome to the Hellspan.

ROLL 3 — THE GRINCH

You return to find the lady still knitting, but your bag looks slumped. You check inside—the laptop is gone. She claims she didn't "see anything" while she was counting stitches. You lose the presentation and the $2,000 laptop. You keep your car and keys.

ROLL 4, 5, 6, 7, 8, or 9 — THE TRAP

You return, and everything is exactly where you left it. The lady smiles. A great outcome, but validates your bad decision with dumb luck. Your brain now registers this risky behavior as safe. You will do it again, and again, and eventually, you will roll a 2. Surviving Russian Roulette doesn't make playing it smart.

ROLL 10 or 11 — THE ABANDONMENT

You return to find the lady gone. She got bored or had to leave. Your bag and laptop have been sitting unattended in a crowded shop for 2 minutes. You get a massive spike of cortisol and a panic attack. You trusted a stranger to care about your property as much as you do. They don't.

ROLL 12 — THE GUARDIAN ANGEL:

You return to find the lady laying on the ground cowering in pain. A teenager tried to grab your bag but the old lady physically stopped a theft. You buy her a coffee after she refuses ambulance care. You used up a lifetime of luck in 3 minutes.

#6– OUTCOME: THE HIGH SCHOOL REUNION

Despite having read this book, you ego cannot stand rolling up to the hotel in your mom's minivan and you buy the BMW. Roll the dice and live in the skin you've sewn.

ROLL 2— THE FLUKE

The BMW acts as a placebo for your confidence. You walk into the reunion like a king, network with a wealthy alum, and land a sales job paying $150K. You pay off the car and move out. (Note: Death Deck, dumb luuck, don't count on it happening again.)

ROLL 3, 4 or 5— THE INVISIBLE MAN

You pull up to the valet stand, ready to turn heads... and nobody is there. Everyone is already inside at the open bar, pounding Coors Light. You spent $58,000 to impress a valet parker named Steve. You spend the night anxious about the payments.

ROLL 6— THE REPO EMBARRASSMENT

You make a grand entrance, and for 4 hours, you feel like a god. Three months later, the money runs out. The car is repossessed in your parents' driveway while the neighbors gawk in sympathy. Your credit score craters from 810 to 460. You don't recover until 36 and wait until 45 to buy a house.

ROLL 7— THE STATISTIC PROBABILITY

A few people see the car and say nothing, only to talk about their kids. That's it. That was the dopamine hit you bought. Now you are stuck with 59 more $799 payments, cementing your residency in your parents' basement until you are nearly 30.

ROLL 8, 9, 10 or 11— THE 30K MILLIONAIRE

You get the car, but the gas and insurance eat your remaining cash. You can't afford to buy anyone a drink at the reunion. Later, you can't keep a girlfriend because you can't afford dinner dates. They quickly realize you are a "30K millionaire"— all hood ornament, no engine.

ROLL 12— THE GHOST

The car works! You impress your high school crush, and she agrees to a date next week. On the date, she asks what you do for a living. When you stutter, she realizes you're an unemployed fraud living with your mom. She blocks your number before the appetizer arrives. You still have 59 payments left.

#7–OUTCOMES: FOMO, THE COUNTERFEIT HARD

You ignored the red flags and bought the stock anyway. Roll the dice to see if the market punishes your stupidity.

ROLL 2—THE JACKPOT

Your $25K turns into $50K. Low-ground, dumb luck. Genius? Nope, you will likely lose it all ROLL you HODL (let it ride), or on your next Treason decision.

ROLL 3 or 4—THE RUIN

Your $25K turns into $1K.

ROLL 5 or 6— THE BAGHOLDER

Your $25K turns into $5K. You are back to where you started 4 years ago.

ROLL 7 or 8—THE CRASH

Your $25K turns into $11K. You are paralyzed by loss aversion.

ROLL 9 or 10— THE BLEED

Your $25K turns into $19K. You refuse to sell, praying it comes back.

ROLL 11— THE TEASE

Your $25K turns into $27K. You hold, waiting for more.

ROLL 12— THE DEATH DECK

:Your $25K is suspended by the SEC. Value: $0.

#8–OUTCOMES: THE PRISON CHOICE (JOB OR FINANCIAL)

SCENARIO A: I KEPT THE JOB!

You chose the counterfeit Hard. You protected your ego, your Alpha status, and your $150k, but you surrendered your weekends, your marriage, and your youth to a stagnant industry.

ROLL 2—THE ARCHITECT

The dying industry miraculously rebounds. The firm gets acquired, and you are handed a massive retention bonus. You cash out at age 30, and your wife somehow tolerated the absence. You are rich and still married.

ROLL 3 or 4—THE WARNING SHOT

You keep hitting your numbers, but the stress compounds. Your wife issues an ultimatum after you miss your child's first steps because of a Thursday afternoon recharge. The marriage survives, but it's on life support. You eventually quit, and your marriage rebounds.

ROLL 5 or 6—THE PRISONER

You plateau. The $150k stagnates while inflation quietly eats your purchasing power. You are chronically exhausted, reliant on caffeine and antacids, and your kid refers to you as "that guy who sleeps on Thursdays." You barely see your wife.

ROLL 7 or 8—THE DEFAULT CRASH

The stagnant industry finally contracts. Your pay is slashed to $100k, but the 60-hour grind remains mandatory. Eventuality arrives: your wife files for divorce because she's effectively a single mother anyway. You now pay alimony based on a $150k lifestyle while earning a fraction of it.

ROLL 9 or 10—THE BLEED

Burnout hits you like a freight train. Your performance drops, and you are stripped of your top salesman status. The mortgage suffocates you. You medicate the exhaustion with alcohol or infidelity. You lose the job and the family.

ROLL 11—THE TEASE

You get a $10,000 raise. It feels like a massive victory, validating your grind. You immediately upgrade your car to celebrate, making the golden handcuffs even heavier. You are trapped forever.

ROLL 12—THE DEATH DECK

The 60-hour chronic stress triggers a massive health crisis (heart attack or stroke at age 28). You are permanently disabled or dead. You traded your one life for a capped paycheck in a dying industry.

SCENARIO B: I ACCEPTED THE NEW JOB!

You Chose Hard. You executed the Truth Translation, paid the $29,000 "freedom tax," swallowed your Alpha-dog pride, and walked into the unknown to buy back your life.

ROLL 2—THE ARCHITECT

You dominate the new industry. Within two years, you obliterate the average and hit the $250k ceiling. You work strictly 40 hours. Your marriage thrives, you are a present father, and you achieve financial independence by age 40. You won the war.

ROLL 3 or 4—THE RUIN

Those "bean counter" layoffs you heard about in the parking lot? They were a red flag. The company's management collapses, and they go bankrupt. You are laid off six months in, with a new baby and zero income.

ROLL 5 or 6—THE MARRIAGE DIVIDEND

You struggle to learn the new industry. For the first two years, you only hit the $80k base. Finances are incredibly tight, forcing you to downsize your house. However, you are home every weekend, and your marriage has never been stronger. It's a financial struggle, but a relational victory.

ROLL 7 or 8—THE CALCULATED CLIMB

You hit the exact mathematical average the Canary Question revealed. You make $121,000. The $29k pay cut stings initially, but you budget, adapt, and never miss a weekend with your kid. The Truth Translation math was perfectly accurate. You are free.

ROLL 9 or 10—THE BLEED THAT WAS WORTH IT

The territory is tougher than expected. You make $100k. The ego hit of no longer being the top dog causes friction and resentment at home, but you eventually swallow your pride, drop the ego, and learn to appreciate the sanity of a 40-hour week. Your marriage eventually improves and becomes the best ever.

ROLL 11—THE TEASE

You make $150k your very first year, perfectly matching your old income, but with weekends off. You feel like a genius and a tactical god.

ROLL 12—THE DEATH DECK

The recruitment firm was duped. The company is a massive fraud (the Mercedes in the parking lot was leased on company credit by the owner's cousin). The SEC raids the building. You are implicated by association, your reputation is torched, and you are blacklisted from the industry.

#9– OUTCOMES: THE NEW JOB AFTERMATH

You accepted the job, but didn't read the contract. Mercedes guy was the owner's brother. A fraud. You made a base salary for months and now, you've quit. What happens next? Roll and find out...

ROLL 2 or 3: THE 10X BUSINESS

You can't find a job after 3 months, but start consulting in the industry you just left. You surprisingly make more money than you did at any other job, and at less hours. You grow it, scale it, and retire a multi-millionaire 7 years later.

ROLL 4 or 5: OUT OF WORK

You're out of work for six months and finances are tight. You need to take a menial job in an industry you don't like. You survive the ordeal and are stronger for it, eventually getting hired in your industry at a fair salary.

ROLL 6 or 8: THE REHIRE

You're rehired back at your old firm, but for less money and under new terms that involve only 40 hour weeks, Monday through Friday. Quitting the other job was a blessing in disguise.

ROLL 9 or 10: THE NEW JOB

You find a new job in a new industry. It pays slightly more and is the same hours. But it is far less stressful and as a result, you and your wife take up pickleball, getting in shape.

ROLL 11: THE BOSS WIFE

While looking for a job, your wife becomes a mega influencer, earning $30K for a 1 minute plug. You become a stay at home dad.

ROLL 12: THE WHISTEBLOWER

You file an SEC complaint with the company you left, complaining of fraud and deception. An investigation reveals you were correct. You're awarded a $2M whistleblower fee for exposing their fraud.

#10–OUTCOMES: THE VAMPIRE CLIENT

ROLL 2: THE TOTAL COLLAPSE

The client explodes, fires you immediately, and badmouths you to their network. You lose 25% of your revenue overnight. Panic sets in. You scramble for low-quality work to fill the gap, but the cash flow crunch is too severe. 9 months later, the agency files for bankruptcy. You are back to square one.

ROLL 3 or 4: THE DELAYED BAND-AID

The client threatens to leave but stays. However, they don't actually change. They behave for a week, then the abuse returns. You tolerate it for another 6 weeks of misery before finally firing them. You wasted 6 more weeks of life. Once they are gone, your team exhales. A month later, you find 3 smaller clients that replace the revenue, but you realize you should have pulled the trigger sooner.

ROLL 5 or 6: THE COMPLIANCE

The client is shocked. They realize they can't bully you anymore. They agree to the new terms. Tension at the firm drops by 50%. The client is still annoying, but manageable. Business continues as usual, but you have reclaimed your self-respect.

ROLL 7: THE POWER SHIFT

The client grumbles, "Well, we pay you enough to work weekends," but you hold the line. They stay because switching agencies is a hassle. By standing up to the bully, you earned their grudging respect. The dynamic shifts from Master/Servant to Peer/Peer. They stop calling on Saturdays because they know you won't answer.

ROLL 8 or 9: THE EFFICIENCY DIVIDEND

You fire the client. It hurts. Revenue dips for 30 days. However, your Account Manager (who was secretly interviewing for other jobs because of this client) decides to stay. With the toxic distraction gone, your team's efficiency on other accounts skyrockets. You don't replace the revenue immediately, but your Net Profit actually increases because you stop burning cash on their chaotic demands.

ROLL 10 or 11: THE UPGRADE

You fire the client. Two weeks later, a referral comes in.Because you have the open capacity (which you wouldn't have had if you kept the vampire), you are able to onboard a new dream client. They pay 20% more than the old client and treat your staff like partners. You traded a headache for a goldmine.

Roll 12: THE 10X LEAP

You fire the client. The relief is instant. Your team morale hits an all-time high. Your rejuvenated Account Manager uses their newfound free time to aggressively hunt new business. Within 2 months, they close 6 new clients, doubling the revenue you lost. The Vampire was the only thing holding your agency back from scaling.

#11– OUTCOME: The Digital Heist

ROLL 2: THE STICKLER

You refuse the refund. A digital flame war ensues online. 6 weeks later, your house burns down.

ROLL 3 or 4 of 5 or 6 or 7 or 8 or 9: THE ACQUIESCENCE:

You refund the customer and never hear from him again.

ROLL 10 or 11 or 12: THE EXTRA COST:

You refuse to refund the customer and never hear from him again, but 6 weeks later you receive a credit card chargeback, losing the money anyway, plus an additional $25 in chargeback fees.

#12– OUTCOMES: "FAMILY FIRST"

ROLL 2: THE BALLER

You accept the partnership and invest $25K. Four years later you cash out with a $100M net worth while meeting the love of your life. You move your family out of the dying town and they are grateful for your decision. The dating partner you left in your hometown has turned into a trainwreck, and you dodged a bullet.

ROLL 3 or 4: THE LIFE CHANGER

You take the new job and invest. After 3 years you liquidate your shares for over $2,000,000. While not "filthy rich" the dollar amount changes your life and allows you to start your own company which then goes on to make tens of millions of dollars.

ROLL 4 or 6: THE GHOST

You decline the job and stay in your hometown. Three months later you lose your job. The partner who you thought was "marriage material" suddenly ghosts you, 4 days after you got pink slipped.

ROLL 7: THE RIGHT CHOICE

You take the new job in the new city and it fails. While you were unable to recover the $25K, you were able to find a job that pays 3X as much as your job back in your home town. Also, your partnership allowed you to meet your soulmate while attending a trade show.

ROLL 8 or 9: THE PIVOT

You take the job and the business barely survives. Three years later, you recover your $25k. While you made a decent salary, the time invested didn't work to your favor. Facing another crossroads, you can take another job that pays 2X more in the city, or move back home.

ROLL 10 or 11: THE LOST LOVE

You take the job and within 18 months, the business has failed. You lose your $25K. You come home with your tail between your legs and your friends are laughing. There person who you were dating has moved on and is married to the town's mayor.

ROLL 12: WHITE PICKET FENCE

You decline the job and stay in your hometown. You rise in the ranks at your job, making the top salary. You get married and buy a house 30 minutes away in a more robust town. While you aren't rich or financially secure, but you live happily ever in a small house you own, white picket fence, and 2 kids.

#13– OUTCOME: THE "I DESERVE IT" TRAP

ROLL 2: THE SMOOTH OPERATOR

You buy the Mercedes. Your newfound confidence gets you a job offer that pays 30% more than what you're making right now. You take the job and it leads to an executive management position. Four years later, the Mercedes is turned in with no harm done, and now you and your spouse own a house.

ROLL 3 or 4: SINGLE, BROKE, AND LOOKING

You buy the and struggle to make payments. Your dream of home ownership flies out the window. The constant financial stress and turmoil in your relationship ends your engagement. You end up single again, living paycheck to paycheck. But hey, at least you look rich.

ROLL 5 or 7: THE MEMORY AND MARRIAGE DIVIDEND

You decline to buy the and instead take a short 5 day vacation with your fiancee as your promotional reward. The vacation is a memorable experience, strengthening the bond with your future spouse. Further, it allows you to save for a down-payment on a home.

ROLL 8 or 9: THE HOMEOWNER

You decline to purchase the Mercedes and start a down payment savings plan with your spouse. Your current beater car runs effectively for another 4 years, ramping up your savings rate. 2 years later, you buy your first home with your spouse. Not only that, you've started saving for your retirement account.

ROLL 10 or 11: THE BETTER JOB

You decline the Mercedes and are thankful you did. 8 months later you're laid off as your company is acquired by a bigger company. Not having the payment allows you to find a better job, with better pay with little disruption to your home life.

ROLL 12: THE BAD NEIGHBORHOOD

You buy the Mercedes and make the payments as scheduled. However, after 4 years of difficult payments, the relationship with your spouse suffers due to the financial duress. With a child expected, the stress ramps up as you still live in a bad apartment on the bad side of town. Additionally, your Mercedes has been broken into twice and your insurance premiums skyrocket. Years later, you're still without a house, without savings, and left with an ailing marriage.

Other Books by MJ DeMarco

Resources to Choose Hard, Live Easy!

MJ's NEWSLETTER: GET LIFE-CHANGING DECISION INTELLIGENCE
https://newslettter.themillionairefastlane.com

MJ'S DISCUSSION FORUM (SINCE 2007!)
https://thefastlaneforum.com/community/

MJ's TELEGRAM GROUP
https://t.me/UnscriptedNetwork

MJs YOUTUBE CHANNEL
https://youtube.com/FastlaneMJ

MJ's PERSONAL BLOG
mjdemarco.com

ORDER BULK OR WHOLESALE COPIES
ViperionPublishingcom